A HORIZON CARAVEL BOOK

THE
SPANISH ARMADA

By the Editors of
HORIZON MAGAZINE

Author
JAY WILLIAMS

Consultant
LACEY BALDWIN SMITH
Professor of History, Northwestern University

Published by American Heritage Publishing Co., Inc.
Book Trade and Institutional Distribution by
Harper & Row

FIRST EDITION
Library of Congress Catalogue Card Number: 66–25994
© 1966 by American Heritage Publishing Co., Inc., 551 Fifth Avenue, New York, New
York, 10017. All rights reserved under Berne and Pan-American Copyright Conventions.
Trademark CARAVEL registered United States Patent Office.

There are a number of HORIZON CARAVEL BOOKS
published each year. Titles now available are:

American Heritage also publishes AMERICAN HERITAGE JUNIOR LIBRARY
books, a similar series on American history. The titles now available are:

FOREWORD

In the summer of 1588 a great body of ships sailed from Spain on a crusade: to restore England to Catholicism. The ensuing events brought a Spanish word, *armada*, into the English language and created a host of exciting legends. Intrepid English sea dogs in tiny ships, it was said, had bravely outfaced the towering galleons of Spain and "drummed the Dons up-Channel." Finally, a storm sent by a vengeful God made the Armada turn tail and wrecked most of that proud fleet on its way home.

Recent research into the facts of the Armada's defeat has shed fresh light on the traditional picture. Although the English were superior sailors, the two fleets were evenly matched. Moreover, the Armada battle emerges as the high point in a forty-year-long cold war between England and Spain. Only when set in the context of a Europe bitterly divided between the Catholic and Protestant faiths can the contest be fully understood. The personalities of Elizabeth I of England and Philip II of Spain and of their commanders—especially that fiery sea dog Francis Drake—are also essential to the story.

The paintings, drawings, and maps that survive from the sixteenth century have provided a treasury of authentic illustrations with the look and feel of real battle. From the same archives comes a provocative footnote to the Armada tale. Supply ships on their way to England's struggling Virginia colony were pressed into service against the Spaniards; by the time they reached Roanoke two years later, every one of the colonists had vanished.

THE EDITORS

The detail opposite from a Vroom painting shows Spanish musketeers aloft firing at the approaching English. Above are the coats of arms of Elizabeth (top) and her chief admiral, Lord Howard.

RIGHT: *In a 1620's engraving the pope and the Devil plot the Armada, but angelic winds disperse it.*
PERMISSION OF THE TRUSTEES OF THE BRITISH MUSEUM

COVER: *Towering over an English ship, the Spanish flagship leads her fleet into the final action.*
NATIONAL MARITIME MUSEUM, GREENWICH

FRONT ENDSHEET: *Robert Adams' map shows the winds and the battles on the Armada's long journey.*
NATIONAL MARITIME MUSEUM, GREENWICH

TITLE PAGE: *The Armada's massive strength is listed on an early seventeenth-century playing card.*
NATIONAL MARITIME MUSEUM, GREENWICH

BACK ENDSHEET: *English fireships attack the Armada in a night view by the Dutch artist Vroom.*
FERDINAND MUSEUM, INNSBRUCK

BACK COVER: *The four English squadrons pursue the Spanish crescent in a detail from Adams' map.*
NATIONAL MARITIME MUSEUM, GREENWICH

Ventorum
Ludibrium

CONTENTS

I   "THE SORROWFUL

The wind, which had been blowing steadily from the sea, changed on that Sunday, October 1, 1567, to a comfortable northeasterly—ideal for taking sailing ships out from the shelter of Plymouth Sound into the English Channel. Six small ships, ranging in size from thirty-three to seven hundred tons, had been waiting in the Catwater over a month for such a day.

Since respect for religious custom meant that they could not sail on the Sabbath, the men aboard were thankful when Monday dawned without a change in the wind. It filled the sails and rippled the brand new banners and pennants as the little fleet sailed in line, with brass cannons gleaming from the open gun ports, and drummers and trumpeters sounding martial fanfares. As they passed alongside the throng of well-wishers waving from Plymouth Hoe, the sailors crowded to the sides of the ships, and the guns fired a salute, which was answered by peals of church bells from the town. Then, as the clamor of the bells died away behind them, the sailors turned back to their regular tasks, and the expedition's leader ordered his ships to set their course southwest for the open sea. Of all the 408 men on board, he alone knew exactly where they were going.

John Hawkins, gentleman of Devon, capable seaman, and prosperous merchant, flew the royal standard of England at the mainmast of his flagship, the *Jesus of Lübeck*. He also displayed his own personal crest—granted him by Queen Elizabeth after his previous and most profitable voyage—a Negro bound with a cord.

Three days out from Plymouth, Hawkins summoned his captains on board the *Jesus*. For the first time he told

In Elizabeth's reign Plymouth served as departure port for many daring sea expeditions. The 1591 map at right shows the maze of inlets that make the sound such a sheltered harbor. At the extreme right, three ships are lying —like Hawkins' fleet—below "cat downe" in the broad bay of the Catwater.

VOYAGE"

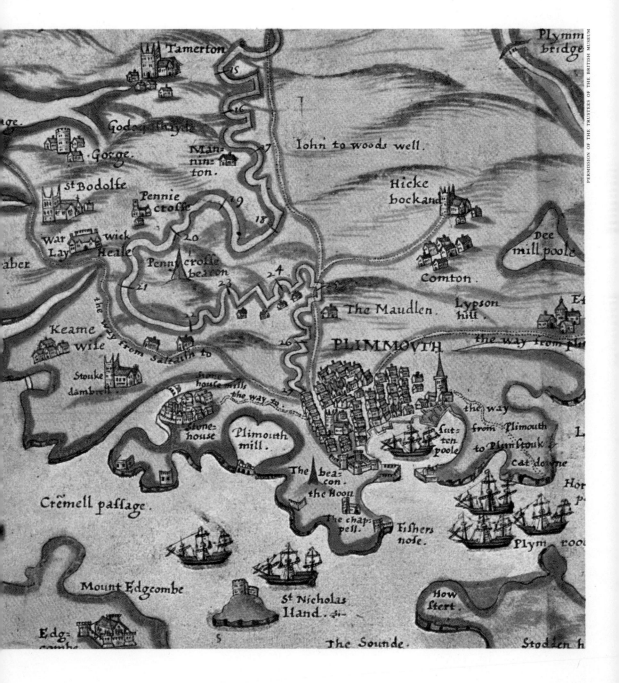

Natives from Guinea, like the men in the engraving above, formed most of Hawkins' cargoes of slaves. So successful were his voyages that the queen allowed him to add the crest of a "demi-Moor bound with a cord" to his coat of arms (below).

them where the ships were bound and what they were going to do. Their first destination was the Portuguese-dominated coast of West Africa, where they would trade with the natives for ivory and gold. Then they would sail to the West Indies and barter their bales of fine woolen cloth and taffeta and their crates of metal goods for the sugar, hides, pearls, and spices that the Spanish colonists would give in exchange.

The most important task of all, however, would be the purchase or capture on the Guinea coast of as many Negro slaves as Hawkins' ships could hold. The Negroes would be the most valuable part of the cargo once the Englishmen reached the West Indies. African slaves were in great demand by the Spanish settlers, who had almost exterminated the native Indian population by using them as forced labor on their plantations and farms. The colonists, quite unprepared to do manual work themselves, could never get enough slaves to meet their needs and were willing to pay extremely high prices for them.

Although Hawkins had no official license from the king of Portugal to collect slaves, nor from the king of Spain to offer them for sale, he did possess articles from the queen of England giving him permission to make the voyage. These he showed to his captains. Then, he appointed a rendezvous at the Canary Islands, 1,750 miles southwest of Plymouth, and dismissed the men to their commands.

Although he was still only thirty-five years old, Hawkins had already made two slaving voyages between the coast of Guinea and the West Indies. The first, in 1562, had been carefully planned and was brilliantly successful. His last trip, in 1564, had brought a profit of 60 per cent to its investors, among whom was the queen herself. This time, she had again taken a share and had contributed two ships from her navy, the 700-ton *Jesus of Lübeck* and the 300-ton *Minion*. The other shareholders were noblemen high in the queen's favor and respectable merchants.

Few people in the sixteenth century thought that slave trading was morally wrong. There was nothing in the Bible that seemed to condemn the practice of selling other human beings, and indeed many people did not even regard Negroes and Indians as human at all. Hawkins could command his men to "serve God daily, love one another, preserve your victuals, beware of fire, and keep good company" with a clear conscience.

A high-minded and religious man, he set forth in hopes of honor and profit from his third voyage to the New

World. Later he was to write of it: "If all the miseries and troublesome affairs of this sorrowful voyage should be perfectly and thoroughly written, there should need a painful man with his pen, and as great a time as he had that wrote the lives and deaths of the Martyrs." Even so, Hawkins could not have foreseen the full extent of these "troublesome affairs" or that this venture was to prove a turning point in the relationship between England and Spain and was to lead to one of history's most famous battles.

Columbus' voyage across the Atlantic in 1492 had opened a great age of discovery. Ships had rounded the tip of Africa to find a sea route to India; the outlines of the two American continents had begun to emerge from the mists of uncertainty; and Magellan had passed through the strait that bears his name, just north of South America's Cape Horn, en route to the first circumnavigation of the globe. Rich native empires in Mexico and Peru had been toppled, and their vast realms opened to settlement. Daring explorers pressed the search for new El Dorados, and traders established commercial routes across the Atlantic to the Caribbean and to the Indian and Pacific oceans.

The Jesus of Lübeck *made an impressive flagship, although she was old and unseaworthy.*

Most of these voyages had been made under the Spanish or the Portuguese flag, and Pope Alexander VI had rewarded these two adventurous and Catholic nations by dividing the earth between them. A line drawn on the map between the forty-first and forty-fourth meridians west of Greenwich gave the West—Mexico, the Caribbean Islands, and all of South America (except Brazil, to which Portugal later laid claim)—to Spain. The East—Africa, India, Sumatra, Java, and the rest of the Orient save for the Philippines—was Portugal's share. Ships crammed with silver, gold, pearls, silks, and spices sailed home to fill the treasuries of the Spanish and Portuguese kings with fantastic riches. And most of this wealth spilled right out again to pay for the defense and maintenance of their vast colonial possessions.

But Europe, of course, did not consist solely of Spain and Portugal. Italy was a collection of separate states, with seagoing interests chiefly contained by the shores of the Mediterranean. Germany, like Italy, did not yet exist as a unified nation. It was torn by continuous religious struggles on land after Martin Luther had defied the Catholic Church, and the tide of the Protestant Reformation spread from one principality to another. A powerful group of north German merchants, called the Hanseatic League, controlled all the sea trade out of the Baltic, but the league was not especially interested in expansion outside Europe. The Netherlands, as part of Spain's empire, was still without a national identity and had to follow the Spanish lead.

Two other powers, however, had been left out of the partition of the world outside Europe, and both resented it. They were France and England.

The French were not quick to take on New World trade or colonies, but they soon grew eager to share in the wealth that was flowing across the seas. In 1523 a squadron of French privateers in the Atlantic captured several Spanish vessels homeward bound with treasure from Mexico. At once, like sharks drawn to the smell of blood, other French ships swarmed to the Azores, the mid-Atlantic islands where the treasure fleets broke their journey, to pick up

prizes. Soon they were sailing right across to the West Indies, raiding the coast towns and looting Spanish ships. It was a logical extension of the conflict that raged hot and cold between Spain and France for the mastery of Europe. And, since most of the privateer captains were French Protestants, or Huguenots, they had a religious excuse for pillaging the property of Catholic Spain.

Matters were different with England, however, for England and Spain had been allies for nearly eighty years. Queen Mary, the Catholic daughter of Henry VIII, had made that long alliance stronger by marrying Philip of Spain in 1554. But they had no children, and when Mary died in 1558, her half-sister, Elizabeth, became queen, and Protestantism again became England's national religion.

A 1502 Portuguese chart includes the line drawn by the pope (left) dividing the world between "castella & portuguall." The New World is vaguely defined, although the map outlines Europe and Africa quite accurately. At center, right, is an unmistakable Red Sea.

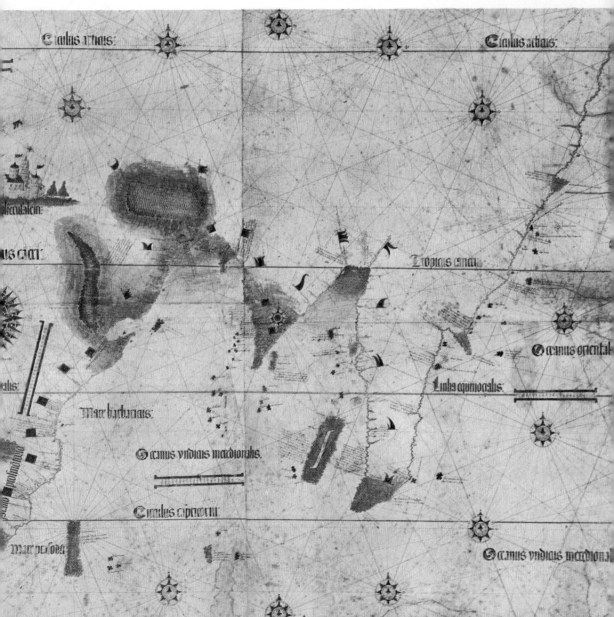

In a miniature painted around 1500 Hanseatic League merchants call at a Russian port. By mid-century English seamen had broken the league's monopoly of Baltic trade.

A new age began in 1558. Slowly, carefully, subtly, Elizabeth began to encourage England's growth as a European power. She could not break off the alliance with Spain at once, for England was not yet strong enough to do so. But she could, and did, support the voyages of her merchant sea captains, and she was able to add money to her scanty treasury by taking shares in some of their ventures. Little by little, English power at sea began to grow, along with a spirit of adventure.

During Mary's reign, English sailors had voyaged to the West African coast and traded with the native rulers despite the monopoly Portugal was supposed to hold there. Philip of Spain, foreseeing that the trading might soon spread to the Spanish-held areas on the other side of the Atlantic, had persuaded Mary to forbid this traffic. But soon after Elizabeth came to the throne, her chief minister told the Spanish ambassador that the pope "had no right to partition the world and to give and take kingdoms to whomever he pleased."

While the queen assured the Spanish and Portuguese ambassadors that she had ordered her subjects not to trade with any area under the actual dominion of the king of Portugal, she knew, and the ambassadors knew, that the Portuguese occupation of West Africa was far from being an effective one. So Englishmen once again sailed down to the Gold Coast, taking pains not to trade in the immediate area of the four or five forts that Portugal maintained along a 2,000-mile-long coastline. Only now the merchant fleets included the queen's own ships, and if the voyage showed profits, a slice went to the Crown. Other English merchant-sailors, seeking a northeast passage to the fabled land of Cathay, or China, succeeded in opening up trade with Russia. Still others spent fortunes and even lost their lives in looking for a northwest passage across North America to the Orient.

Long before his 1567 voyage, John Hawkins, a shrewd and thoughtful man, had begun to look toward the west and to have hopes of legal trade with the wealthy islands of the Caribbean. While in general only Spaniards were allowed to trade in Spanish possessions, some foreigners had been granted licenses. But the colonists had more goods to sell than the licensed traders could handle. In addition the settlers were subject to constant harassment by privateers because there were not enough Spanish ships or soldiers to defend them. Hawkins may have hoped that by offering his services and those of his ships to help the Spanish governors

BY PERMISSION OF THE DUKE OF BEDFORD, WOBURN ABBEY

A youth full of illness and injustices left its mark on Mary Tudor's life. At thirty-eight she married Philip of Spain, a widower of twenty-seven, but the union brought her little joy and no heir. Mary's rigidly Catholic beliefs sent 300 Protestants to the stake before she died in 1558, the year in which the portrait of the royal couple at right was painted.

in controlling this piracy he could win an official trading license from the king of Spain. Failing that he could do a good business anyway; his previous voyages proved that.

Hawkins himself and his brother William, who managed the family affairs from the Plymouth office, had contributed four ships to the new expedition. These were the *William and John*, 150 tons, the *Swallow*, 100 tons, the *Judith*, a 50-ton bark, and the tiny 33-ton *Angel*.

Although the queen's two ships were much more impressive looking vessels, and were heavily armed, both had in fact been condemned as not worth repairing for naval use. The *Jesus of Lübeck* had been bought from the Hanseatic League by King Henry VIII twenty-three years earlier, and although Hawkins had done his best to put her in seaworthy shape, her timbers were rotten. The arrangement by which the queen loaned the ships was that Hawkins must repair them and fit them out at his own cost. If the voyage made a profit, the queen's portion would be based

17

John Hawkins' character—shrewd, upright, and scrupulous—can be glimpsed in this portrait of him at forty-fou

18

on the valuation of her ships: £2,000 for the *Jesus*, and for the *Minion* perhaps half of that. Hawkins knew they were overvalued, but their guns were good, and they were royal ships with the appearance of power.

Off the northern coast of Spain the ships were separated by a violent storm. A seaman on board the *Jesus* wrote later that she "opened in the stern, aft, and leaks broke out in divers places in her . . . in the stern the leak was so great that into one place there was thrust 15 piece of baize to stop the place." For four days Hawkins had his crew laboring at bailing the ship and plugging up the leaks, and when he finally told them all to pray for their lives because only God could save them, not one of his men "could refrain his eyes from tears." Finally the wind dropped, and they limped into the Canary Islands rendezvous.

Amazingly, none of the other ships had been lost, and after taking on fresh food and water and making some repairs to the *Jesus*, they went on toward Africa.

They reached Cape Vert, on the coast of present-day Senegal, on November 18, and landed, expecting to capture many slaves. Instead they ran into an ambush. Warriors armed with bows and hide shields attacked them with showers of arrows. The English had to return to their ships with twenty wounded men and only nine captives. Worse still, the native arrows had been poisoned, and within a few days, eight of the wounded developed lockjaw and died. Captain Hawkins himself had an arrow in his arm and was said to have escaped death only by rubbing a clove of garlic over his wound to draw the poison from it. After this unsuccessful venture they were glad to sail on toward Sierra Leone, skirmishing along the coast as they went.

On the way south they met with a 150-ton ship commanded by a Captain Bland, a French privateer who had captured the vessel from the Portuguese. Hawkins seized the ship and placed in charge of her a young cousin of his named Francis Drake, who had been sailing as an officer on the *Jesus*. Before long, however, Bland decided to join the expedition voluntarily. He and his men were reinstated in his ship, and Drake was given command of the *Judith*.

By Christmastime they had obtained only 150 Negroes and were growing short of time; the voyage across the West Indies would take two months, and they must plan to leave again for England before the hurricane season in July. Then a native king of Sierra Leone asked Hawkins for help. He planned to attack the fortified town of a rival chief and was prepared to offer the Englishmen all the prisoners they

could take in return for their aid. Hawkins agreed and joined in the assault.

After two days of hard fighting, the town was captured and burned. Hawkins' men took 250 prisoners, and the African king got 600. Hawkins expected to take his share of these too, but during the night the king marched off with his captives, leaving the English slave traders to complain bitterly about other people's lack of morals.

However, they now had enough slaves to try for the

Above, Hawkins' Caribbean route in 1568 is superimposed on a map made that year. Leaving Dominica (1), he visited Borburata (2), Rio de la Hacha (3), Santa Marta (4), and Cartagena (5). Making for the channel between Cuba and Florida, he was blown west to San Juan de Ulua (6). Fleeing north, he left half his crew on the coast of Texas (7) before turning home.

Caribbean, and on February 7, 1568, they set sail westward, reaching the Lesser Antilles by the end of March. After one or two stops for food and water, they came to Borburata, now known as Puerto Cabello, Venezuela.

At this port they learned that King Philip of Spain had strictly prohibited all trade with foreigners as a result of Hawkins' earlier trips. They also learned that the governor, whose job it was to enforce the ban, was away in another part of his province. Hawkins at once sent letters asking for permission to trade, and while waiting for the governor's reply, he began doing business with the eager merchants of Borburata anyway.

The answer, when it finally came, was a courteous "No," but by then Hawkins' trading arrangements were well established, and it was two months before he made for his next port of call. This was Rio de la Hacha, farther west along the South American coast, and Francis Drake with the *Judith* and the *Angel* went ahead to open negotiations.

In a sense, this was Drake's first independent command. He was in his middle twenties, a stocky, bright-eyed young man, full of curiosity and eager to make money. The son of a Devonshire preacher, he had been brought up on the water—literally so, because his family had been so poor they had had to live aboard an abandoned hulk. As a boy he had been apprenticed to the captain of a small boat that traded between England and the coast of the Netherlands, and he had learned his job so well that when the captain died, he bequeathed his boat to young Drake.

In 1566, Drake had joined a West Indies expedition financed by the Hawkinses. He and his commander, however, had been cheated out of most of their cargo—and the Hawkinses of their investment—by the governor of the same Rio de la Hacha he was approaching in June, 1568.

It may have been out of personal revenge—since Hawkins had always been scrupulously careful not to give offense to the Spanish authorities—that Drake shot a cannon ball clean through the governor's house and captured a dispatch boat at Rio de la Hacha. Hawkins then came up with the rest of the fleet, landed his musketeers, and chased the townspeople into the woods. However, the Spaniards did need laborers, and Hawkins did want to make sales. Several polite letters were exchanged, Hawkins agreed to pay the usual 7.5 per cent duty (which could really be called graft), and matters were settled agreeably for both sides with the sale of two hundred slaves.

It was now early July, and Hawkins had to get out of

21

This drawing of a burdened Indian slave is from the sketchbook of an official who chronicled the brutal extension of the Spanish empire.

the Caribbean before the hurricane season. He did some business at Santa Marta, where the local authorities aided him in staging the "capture" of the town so that the governor could claim he had been forced by the Englishmen to trade with them. After a couple of pleasant weeks, they went on to Cartagena. There the situation was very different.

Cartagena was the chief port of the Spanish Main, or mainland of South America, and the regular assembly point for the treasure fleet that sailed once each year in convoy to Spain. It was well fortified, and the governor steadfastly refused to have anything to do with the English intruders. Regretfully, because he still had some slaves to sell and had hoped to take in more supplies for the long transatlantic voyage, Hawkins turned his ships for home.

He had waited a little too long. Off the coast of Cuba, on August 12, his fleet was caught in a violent tropical storm. By the time it was over, the *William and John* had disappeared (she eventually turned up in Ireland the following February), and although the smaller ships were in good enough shape, the old *Jesus of Lübeck* had suffered terribly. With a damaged rudder, several spars missing, and all hands pumping out the water that poured in through the open seams, Hawkins' ship sought desperately for a landing place on the Florida coast. He would have done better to abandon her, but she belonged to the queen, and as an honorable man he was determined to save her if he could. Then another gale came roaring up and scattered his fleet to the southwest. When the storm ended, Hawkins learned from a passing ship that the only harbor he had any chance of reaching was that of San Juan de Ulua.

San Juan de Ulua was small and shabby, but it was the only safe anchorage along the gulf coast of New Spain, as Mexico was then known. Each fall it was visited by a fleet bringing stores and equipment from Spain. In exchange, the ships took on board silver and gold, dyes and hides, that the Mexican settlers had accumulated over the months for King Philip's treasuries and for the rich merchants of Seville. Then, heavily armed and with a warship escort, they would sail to Havana and there rendezvous with the other treasure fleet from Cartagena before going on across the Atlantic.

Hawkins was putting his neck into a possible noose, but he had to repair his ships and replenish his stores. On September 16, flying the royal standard, his fleet sailed into San Juan de Ulua. The garrison mistook it for the treasure fleet, due any day, and welcomed it with a salute.

The Andean "mountain of silver" at Potosi, seen in 1584 (right), was a major source of Spanish wealth. The primitive refinery in the foreground, supplied with ore by relays of llamas, produced enough bullion in its first 160 years of operation to triple Europe's silver supply.

After the first panic of discovering their mistake, the Spaniards were calmed by Hawkins, who assured them that he would pay for whatever he took. Everything, it seemed, could be settled quietly.

But Hawkins' "sorrowful voyage" was far from over. The next morning a lookout reported thirteen great ships on the horizon, running for the harbor before a brisk wind. The treasure fleet had arrived.

English ships had no business in Spanish harbors, and particularly when a fortune in treasure was to be loaded. The official Spanish view was that they were pirates and should be treated as such. For his own safety, Hawkins had to take some measures of defense.

The mouth of the harbor was guarded by a shore battery of a dozen cannons mounted on a breakwater. He dispatched a couple of boatloads of men to seize the guns and cover the harbor entrance. Then he sent a boat out to the Spaniards with the message that they would only be allowed to enter the harbor if they agreed to his conditions.

23

He must be permitted to buy food and water and to repair his ships in peace. He would hold the breakwater and its battery until he left. And ten hostages would be given from each side to prevent treachery. Secretly, Hawkins knew that whatever happened he would have to let the Spaniards enter. If he forced them to stay outside their own harbor, at the mercy of any storm, it would be as much an act of war as if he deliberately fired at them. The queen would never forgive a captain flying her standard who put her in such a position while England and Spain were still at peace. But he simply had to try the bluff.

To his immense relief, the viceroy of New Spain, Don Martin Enriquez, who was on board the treasure fleet's flagship, agreed to the terms. He sent Hawkins a cordial letter, the agreement was signed, and they exchanged hostages. The Spanish ships came into the harbor and anchored alongside the English.

However, Don Martin Enriquez had no intention whatever of keeping his word. Hawkins had insulted his honor by making intolerable conditions. A bargain struck between a Spanish nobleman and a man whom he thought of as a heretic and a pirate did not exist; so there was no question of breaking faith by ignoring the conditions at his own convenience.

A few days later, the trap was sprung. At the sound of a trumpet, troops from the shore rowed over to the breakwater, rushed the Englishmen guarding the cannons, captured the guns, and turned them on Hawkins' ships. At the same time, the vessels of the treasure fleet opened fire, and a party of Spaniards tried to board the *Minion*.

The first attack was beaten off. Hawkins cut the *Jesus'* moorings, and her longboats towed her into the open harbor where he could bring his own heavy guns to bear upon the Spanish ships. A lucky shot hit one galleon's powder magazine, which exploded with a roar. Another Spanish ship was sunk by a broadside. Smoke billowed up from burning timbers, and splinters flew from cannon balls that plowed along decks and crashed through bulwarks.

Hawkins, cool and calm as always, called for a drink of beer. When it was brought, in a silver cup, he toasted his gunners and drank. As he set the cup down a shot carried it away. "Fear nothing," Hawkins shouted to his men, "for God who has preserved me from this shot will also deliver us from these traitors and villains."

But the combined fire from the captured battery and the galleons was too much for him. The *Judith* and the

In 1590 an Italian engineer made this water-color sketch of the island harbor of San Juan de Ulua. In the foreground is the breakwater where Hawkins' ships tied up alongside the Spanish fleet.

Minion had managed to get out of the harbor, but the *Swallow* and the *Angel* were both sunk. So was the French privateer. The *Jesus*, already in bad shape, had taken the worst punishment from the guns and could not be saved. Hastily, using her as a screen against the gunfire, Hawkins began transferring her supplies and the treasure from the long months of trading into the *Judith* and the *Minion*. Then the Spaniards set one of their own ships on fire, and as she came coasting down upon the English, men jumped wildly from the decks of the *Jesus* onto the *Minion*. Hawkins him-

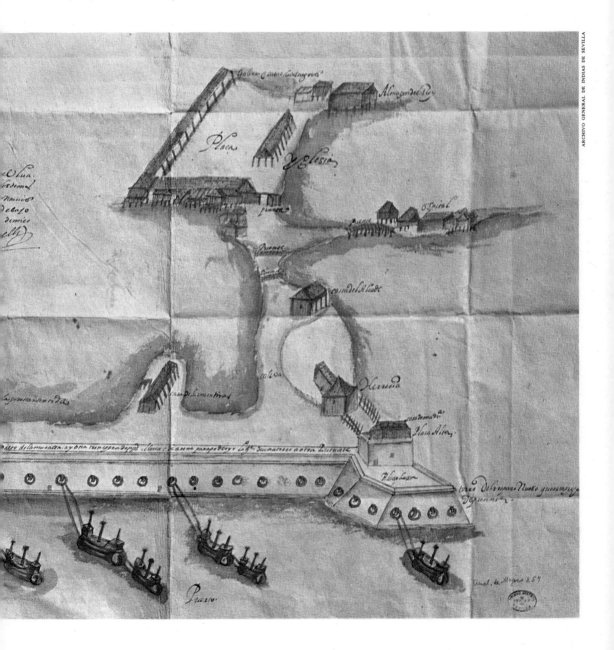

self barely clambered over the *Minion*'s side as she drew off. Behind him he left his wounded, forty-five Negro slaves, and the ten Spanish hostages—unharmed.

The two ships, crowded with survivors, anchored for the night in the lee of a small island out of range of all but the heaviest Spanish guns. During the night a stiff wind got up, and by morning Drake's ship, the *Judith*, had disappeared—"forsook us in our great misery," as Hawkins later wrote. What happened has never been explained. Drake never spoke of it; nor did Hawkins, after this one reference, ever seem to hold it against him. The facts are that Drake arrived in England at last on January 20, 1569, after a voyage of which nothing is known, and five days later Hawkins, in the *Minion*, also arrived after a journey filled with dreadful sufferings.

Of the two hundred men who left San Juan de Ulua with Hawkins, perhaps fifteen survived to sail again. By the end of their three-month ordeal, their only food was leather hides stewed into a semblance of soup. In October, with supplies already pitifully short, one hundred of Hawkins' men had preferred to take the chance of being put ashore near what is now Corpus Christi, Texas. Some were killed by Indians; some found their way to Mexico, where most died after being interrogated as heretics by the Spanish Inquisition. Three, amazingly, escaped and eventually reached home after incredible adventures.

What had happened at San Juan de Ulua meant that the relationship between England and Spain could never again be the same. To the narrowly upright mind of King Philip of Spain, and hence to his councilors, the Spanish position was perfectly defensible. The Caribbean was rightly Spanish territory, allotted by the pope, and had to be controlled through regular licensing laws. All of Hawkins' expeditions had been violations of these laws, but only on the last one had Spain been in a position to do anything about it. No one felt that Don Martin Enriquez merited anything but praise for the punishment he had meted out to a Protestant pirate—to the Catholic Spaniards, Protestants had no more rights than Hawkins and his men allowed the wretched Africans they took into slavery.

To Hawkins and Drake, who had intended honest trading and had been treated like pirates, revenging the treachery of San Juan de Ulua became the occupation of their lifetimes. Drake even considered that he had a private feud with the king of Spain. Staunch Protestants both, they believed they were upholding true religion by their actions.

Storms added a new hazard to the ordeal of Hawkins' starving crew: clambering high into their ship's rigging, like the mariners in this detail, they had to reef the sails.

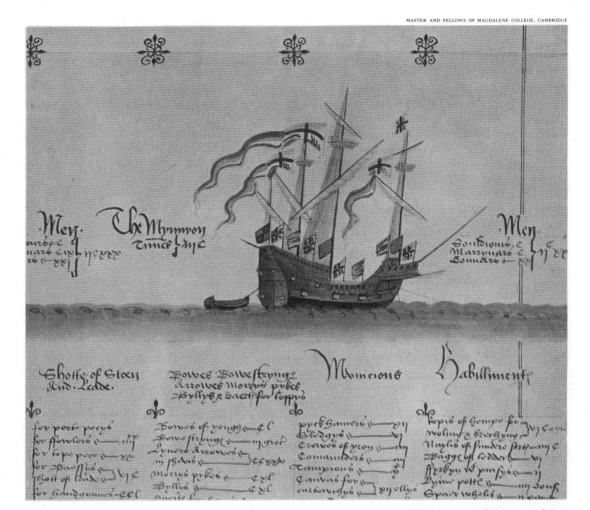

The Minion, *with banners flying, is depicted above in a list of Royal Navy ships built for Henry VIII. The galleon was thirty years old, and was "spent and rotten," by the time she brought home the few survivors of the "sorrowful voyage."*

"And if it shall not please the Queen's Majesty to meddle in this affair," wrote Hawkins' brother William to Sir William Cecil, Elizabeth's chief minister, "yet that she would give her subjects leave to meddle with them [the Spaniards] by law, and then I trust we should not only have recompense to the uttermost, but also do as good service as is to be devised with so little cost. And I hope to please God best therein, for they are God's enemies!"

Elizabeth did not give "leave to meddle" by law, but increasingly she permitted private adventurers to seek recompense and to fill their own pockets—and hers—at Spain's expense. The long alliance between England and Spain was really over, whatever rulers and politicians might do or say on the surface of things. Although neither Queen Elizabeth nor King Philip wanted war, it would slowly become clear that peace was no longer possible.

27

CAROL

CAROL

20 Orat. Hisp.   Cancel. Concil.   19

LEOPOLDO I CÆSARI AVGVSTO.

cælata Oecumenici Tridentini Concilij historia, ex debito magis quàm voto Tuæ sacratur Maiestati: neminem quippe latet, Diue;
Tuos Carolum V. et Ferdinandum I quorum et virtutis et sceptri maximus es hæres, sacram hanc Synodum à Romanis Pontificibus
nis votis expetijsse, impetrasse, propugnasse fortissime, donec extitialia Europæ monstra Luterus et Caluinus veritatis telo conciderent
ata Accedit Sapientissimorum P.P. Censorum non nisi apud illam Maiestatem collocandum, cuius in pectoris sacrario Cana
entia orbis testimonio domicilium fixit. Sic cogitas, sic loqueris, sic denig̃ agis, ut annos consilio, omnium admirationem ac
Diuino indolis auguste gente longissime anteuertas. Admitte igitur hoc non tam munus Seruorum Postremi quàm
atorio demu; ꝑ æternà et admitte illæ qua tuos faciscentem malis orbem, exhilaras superstite et firmas.

28

II

EUROPE DIVIDED

To Hawkins, Drake, and their fellow seamen, the treachery at San Juan de Ulua may have seemed the major event of 1567–68. But these years also brought to Europe significant changes that in the end were even more responsible than the San Juan engagement for setting England onto a collision course with Spain.

The sixteenth century was a time of great religious ferment in Europe. In the fifty years since Martin Luther first challenged Church authority, Protestantism had emerged as a vital threat to the universally held Roman Catholic faith. Dominated by popes and clergy who often seemed more interested in material comforts than in spiritual matters, the Catholic Church had indeed grown slack and corrupt. After the Council of Trent at mid-century had decided that compromise or reconciliation between Protestants and Catholics was impossible, the Church counterattacked, both by reform within itself and by outright military means. To the Church, heresy was not only morally wrong; it was criminal and had to be stamped out.

European rulers, Protestant and Catholic, held that all the inhabitants of a country must practice the same religion as their prince; any man who held a different religious belief was committing high treason. If he joined a hostile religious group, it became rebellion and often resulted in open war. Kings ruled by divine right, and God-fearing subjects must obey them.

Protestants hoped to fear and serve God better by organizing themselves into well-disciplined and morally upright congregations. John Calvin had established in Geneva a model state governed on strict religious principles that

In 1517 his famous protest against abuses in the Church made Martin Luther (above) leader of the religious revolution sweeping Europe. By the 1550's Church dignitaries meeting at the Council of Trent (opposite) had reformed Catholicism but had outlawed Luther's followers as heretics.

29

strongly appealed to men all over Europe who were eager to find a satisfying faith. The questing spirit of the Renaissance was not only working outward, drawing men to adventure far afield, but inward, leading men to search for and explore their own potentialities. Calvin's "New Jerusalem" at Geneva seemed a shining example of what could be done by faith and hard work. Successive waves of refugees from the religious wars that were increasingly tearing Europe apart poured into the city, and printers, booksellers, and ministers spread the new faith abroad again to one country after another.

Both sides engaged in the struggle with all the fervor, and the excesses, of a crusade. Led by the pope, Catholics were ready to identify all Protestants as followers of Satan —who was a very real force in the sixteenth century. The Protestants' desire to be free to worship as individuals brought to countries where they were strong a new sense of national identity. A patriotic longing for independence began to mingle with religious conviction as a reason for fighting on behalf of the Protestant Reformation.

There was also a strong desire for material gain. An incredible quantity of riches was flooding into Europe from

An efficient visionary, Calvin recognized that Protestantism needed organization. His strict control made the city of Geneva, seen below in 1548, into "New Jerusalem" for his numerous followers.

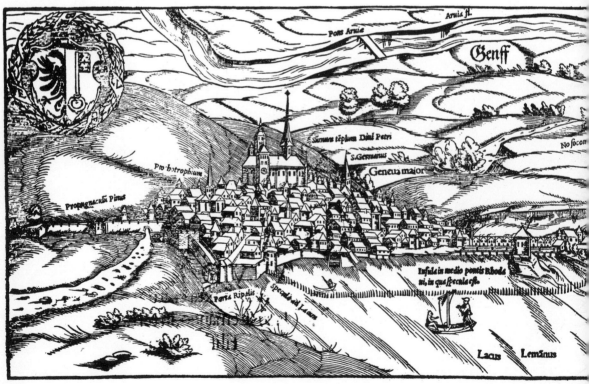

A student sketched John Calvin (above) shortly before the Protestant leader's death in 1564.

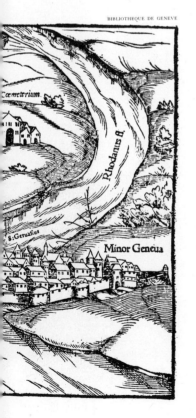

the recently discovered lands to the east and west, and fortunes could be made in the religious wars. Italians and Germans hired themselves out as mercenary soldiers, fighting for whoever offered the best pay; Frenchmen and Englishmen became privateers at sea, robbing Catholic shipping to advance the Protestant cause and lining their own pockets in the process.

In the years 1567–68 the two chief Catholic powers— France and Spain—each faced the existence of an open Protestant rebellion within their territories.

The civil war of 1567–68 was one of a series of draining religious wars in France between the Catholics and the Huguenot followers of Calvin. Beginning in 1562 and continuing intermittently for the rest of the century, the conflict divided and devastated a state already enfeebled by a succession of weak, adolescent kings. To Catherine de Médicis, Queen Mother and Regent of France, the conflict was only one stage in a long and complicated struggle for supremacy that she had to win to preserve the throne for her eighteen-year-old son, Charles IX, and for his two younger brothers. A mother before anything else, she was prepared to compromise and intrigue endlessly, even with the Huguenot leaders, to safeguard her children's position.

To Philip of Spain, the most powerful monarch in the world, the revolt that had broken out in his Netherlands territory in 1566 was a double blow; it was a direct affront to his authority over his widespread empire and a challenge to his responsibility as its spiritual leader. When he inherited the seventeen Netherlands provinces, ten years earlier, he had found them most prosperous but riddled with heresy and obstinately insistent on preserving their ancient rights. Even the Catholic nobles, led by Prince William of Orange, governor of the northern provinces, protested against Philip's repression of Protestantism and requested the restoration of old civil liberties.

Philip was an orderly man who preferred to have in a subordinate province an administration similar to that of his chief kingdom, Castile. He was also devoutly religious, and when Calvinist mobs began desecrating Catholic churches and running wild through the Netherlands cities, he felt it his duty to take severe reprisals. "Rather than make the slightest concession to the detriment of religion," he wrote to the pope, "I would prefer to lose a hundred lives if I had them. I do not care to rule over heretics."

Ignoring the counsel of his more tolerant advisers, he dispatched the Duke of Alva with an army of twenty thou-

This allegory, painted in 1614, portrays the bitter division between Catholics and Protestants that exhausted Europe for well over a century. Protestants crowd the

left bank, Catholics the right, as their leaders in rowboats fish converted souls
out of the river of life. A close inspection will reveal the painter's own religion.

sand men to deal with the rebellion. He had chosen wisely. Alva was leader of the Spanish party in favor of repression in the Netherlands, and he was an able military commander as well. By the end of 1567 he had established martial law through a council dominated by himself and had begun burning or hanging all whom he called rebels and heretics. Thousands of refugees fled the country, spreading horror stories about Alva's "Council of Blood."

Among those who left was Prince William of Orange, who took refuge in lands he owned in Germany. During his years in the northern provinces, which were predominantly Calvinist, Prince William, never more than a nominal Catholic, had found himself increasingly attracted by Protestantism. His reasons for opposing Alva's council, however, were mainly patriotic. He wanted to preserve the unity of the Netherlands.

In 1568 he raised an army in Germany and crossed the frontier to liberate his country from Alva's reign of terror. The campaign was brief. The people of the Netherlands, already disunited, were too cowed to rise up and support Prince William, and he had to abandon his campaign. Alva had a stranglehold on the country. He himself boasted that he executed eighteen thousand people in his attempt to stamp out heresy and the Netherlands' independence along with it.

William tried another approach. He allied himself with the French Huguenots, who had begun to operate a regular privateering campaign out of the port of La Rochelle, in western France. William now offered official commissions to Dutch seamen to strike a blow for Protestantism by attacking Spanish ships. By 1570 there were over a hundred of these "Sea Beggars" sweeping up and down the English Channel, helping themselves to Alva's merchandise and moneybags. They were a mixed bunch: Dutch, French, and English, and the English ports were the main disposal points for booty. King Philip's ships ran the gantlet of Protestant privateers all the way from Spain to the Netherlands, and very few of them got through. Meanwhile, the coffers of Prince William, Queen Elizabeth, and the Huguenot leaders received constant additions of treasure, and men like John Hawkins and his friends were winning a rich recompense for past wrongs—all in the name of religion.

The result of the privateers' outrages was that legal trade between England and Spain was broken off completely. The two countries were still not at war, although

The Duke of Alva (above), Philip II's governor in the Netherlands, spent seven years trying—and failing—to stamp out Protestantism.

Rebellion in the Netherlands was sparked in 1566 by mobs of Calvinists who desecrated and pillaged Catholic churches. In this German engraving, rioters are busy toppling images and smashing windows.

Philip's ambassador to London now began to enter into dangerous intrigues that could lead to hostilities. Their focal point was Elizabeth's cousin, Mary Queen of Scots.

In 1568 Mary had sought refuge in England after being deposed by her people in favor of her infant son, James. Under the care of various Scottish regents, James was being raised as a Protestant, although his mother was a Catholic. A further complication arose from the fact that Mary was also heir to Elizabeth's throne—as long as Elizabeth did not marry and produce an heir of her own. To every Catholic in England, Mary already had a better claim to the crown than Elizabeth. She was the granddaughter of Henry VIII's sister, who had married the king of Scotland, whereas Elizabeth was the offspring of what was—in Catholic eyes—an illegal union between Henry VIII and Anne Boleyn, his second wife.

Mary's claim worried Elizabeth's advisers more than it disturbed the queen herself. Confident of her subjects' personal affection for her and their appreciation of the prosperity her peaceful reign was bringing England, she confined Mary to a northern castle, under close supervision, and began an endless series of negotiations to get the

35

EUROPE AS DIVIDED AMONG THE ROYAL HOUSES

Shetland Islands

NORWAY

SWEDEN

Hebrides

SCOTLAND

Edinburgh

North Sea

DENMARK

Baltic Sea

IRELAND

Dublin

Lubeck

Hamburg

POLAND

ENGLAND

London

Brielle • Delft

Plymouth • • Dover NETHERLANDS

Antwerp

HOLY

Calais

Brussels

ROMAN

English Channel

NASSAU

Luxembourg

EMPIRE

AUSTRIA

Paris

Vienna

FRANCE

Dijon

FRANCHE
COMTE

La Rochelle

Bay of Biscay

SWITZERLAND

Lyons • Geneva

Milan Venice

OTTOMAN

Cape
Finisterre • Corunna

Genoa

EMPIRE

Santander

PAPAL

NAVARRE

STATES

PORTUGAL

Escorial • • Madrid

ARAGON

Barcelona

Rome

Lisbon

SPAIN

Naples • NAPLES

Cape
St.
Vincent

CASTILE

Seville

Balearic Islands

SARDINIA

Lepanto

Cadiz

Strait of Gibraltar

Mediterranean Sea

SICILY

BARBARY STATES

Atlantic Ocean

	POSSESSIONS OF TUDOR KINGS OF ENGLAND		POSSESSIONS OF HAPSBURG KINGS OF SPAIN
	POSSESSIONS OF STUART KINGS OF SCOTLAND		PORTUGAL, ACQUIRED BY SPAIN IN 1580
	POSSESSIONS OF VALOIS KINGS OF FRANCE		POSSESSIONS OF AUSTRIAN HAPSBURGS
	POSSESSIONS OF BOURBON KINGS OF NAVARRE		JURISDICTION OF HOLY ROMAN EMPEROR

FRANCIS & SHAW

Sixteenth-century rulers were preoccupied with marriage—their own or their children's. No woman in those days could hope for a husband unless she brought him a dowry of money or land; princesses' dowries were often whole countries. By elaborate intermarriages kings could acquire possessions and power, but in a period when queens frequently died in childbirth and few of their children survived infancy, any ruler left widowed was forced to remarry almost at once. The map opposite shows how Europe was divided among the chief royal houses around 1568. The chart below, color-keyed to the countries they ruled, gives an idea of their interrelationship.

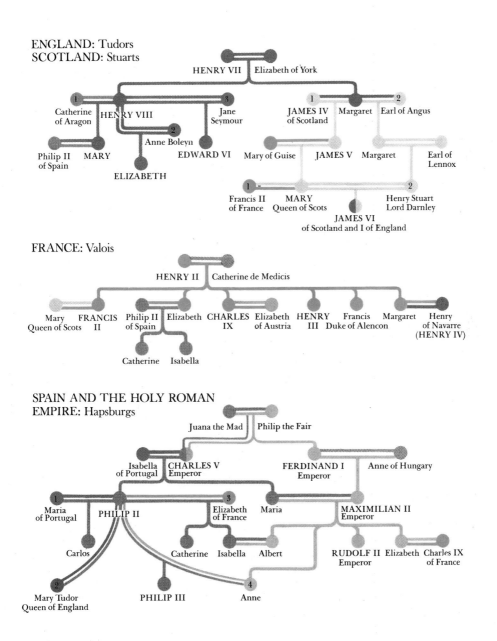

ENGLAND: Tudors
SCOTLAND: Stuarts

HENRY VII | Elizabeth of York

Catherine of Aragon | HENRY VIII | Jane Seymour

JAMES IV of Scotland | Margaret | Earl of Angus

Anne Boleyn

Philip II of Spain | MARY | EDWARD VI | Mary of Guise | JAMES V | Margaret | Earl of Lennox

ELIZABETH

Francis II of France | MARY Queen of Scots | Henry Stuart Lord Darnley

JAMES VI of Scotland and I of England

FRANCE: Valois

HENRY II | Catherine de Medicis

Mary Queen of Scots | FRANCIS II | Philip II of Spain | Elizabeth | CHARLES IX | Elizabeth of Austria | HENRY III | Francis Duke of Alencon | Margaret | Henry of Navarre (HENRY IV)

Catherine | Isabella

SPAIN AND THE HOLY ROMAN EMPIRE: Hapsburgs

Juana the Mad | Philip the Fair

Isabella of Portugal | CHARLES V Emperor | FERDINAND I Emperor | Anne of Hungary

Maria of Portugal | PHILIP II | Elizabeth of France | Maria | MAXIMILIAN II Emperor

Carlos | Catherine | Isabella | Albert | RUDOLF II Emperor | Elizabeth | Charles IX of France

Mary Tudor Queen of England | PHILIP III | Anne

Scots to take Mary back again or otherwise dispose of her.

In the autumn of 1569, however, Elizabeth too faced a civil war in the name of religion. Catholic nobles in the north led a rising against her and attempted to seize Mary and put her on the throne. The revolt was quickly put down, and Mary never fell into rebel hands. But from that time on the chorus of demand that she be eliminated began to swell, and with each new turn of events in the complicated European picture, it became more obvious how dangerous Elizabeth's "guest" really was.

Mary was an unusually charming woman with a gift for winning hearts. Unlike Elizabeth, who governed her country like a man, Mary allowed herself to be ruled by emotion and had lost her kingdom in consequence. Brought up in France and for two years its queen, Mary was always responsive to the interests of her relations there, the extremely powerful Guise family, who had dominated her husband, Francis II, during his brief reign and who continued to dominate his successor, Charles IX. Catherine de Médicis had temporarily succeeded in lessening Guise influence over Charles by a series of alliances with the Huguenot party, but Mary knew as well as Catherine that nothing was ever stable at the court of France. Once the Guises were again in the ascendancy, Mary felt confident that they would rescue her from prison and restore Catholicism in Britain by making her queen of Scotland once more—and of England too.

In the eighteen years Mary was to spend in captivity, she had few activities to pass the time away, save making plans for the future. She was a natural focus for many plots on the part of Catholics in England and in exile abroad, and she is known to have been personally involved in four major attempts to overthrow Elizabeth.

In these plots, however, a stronger ally even than the Guises was necessary. As chief monarch of Europe and leader of the Counter Reformation, Philip of Spain was the obvious person. "Tell your master," Mary wrote secretly to the Spanish ambassador, "that if he will help me, I shall be queen of England in three months and mass shall be said all over the kingdom."

Although Philip recognized Mary as the legitimate claimant to the English throne, he was far from eager to make arrangements to put her on it. Not only was he excessively cautious by nature—admitting his difficulty in making up his mind, he once joked, "Time and I are a match for any other two"—but he realized that the game of

A sixteenth-century painting poses Mary Queen of Scots with her year-old son James, for whom she abdicated the Scottish throne in 1567. The two never met again.

politics required careful manipulation. Religious conflict had given a new pattern and coloring to traditional European relationships, completely realigning old alliances based on trade, habit, and common interests. A precarious balance of power had to be maintained because part of Spain's great strength lay in France's present disunity and consequent weakness. Putting Mary on the English throne would give France, through her, all too much weight in Europe. Heretic though Elizabeth was, it really suited Philip better to have her in control of England. She also understood how to play the game of politics to ensure that no one country—except one's own—became too powerful.

Philip arranged his manipulations through a vast network of spies—so many, in fact, that they sometimes spied upon one another without knowing that they were all working for the same king. They sent in their reports, and Philip, who was a born clerk, read them, annotated them, corrected their spelling, and filed them away. In his own good time he acted upon the information they contained.

Elizabeth too used spies, but she had an even more effective way of keeping abreast of the situation in Europe —the offer of herself as a possible marriage partner. At the start of her reign, with the Protestant religion newly re-established in England after years of persecution, a Catholic cousin of King Philip's was the top candidate. Once the pattern of the new reign had been set, Elizabeth's agile mind found good reasons for toying with a marriage proposal from France.

Catherine de Médicis, anxious to get a crown for each of her children, offered first her third son, Henry, and then her youngest son, Francis, Duke of Alençon, as possible suitors for a queen who was old enough to be their mother. Through years of protracted negotiations, Elizabeth encouraged the idea as a method of averting a possible alliance between French Huguenots and Dutch Protestants, which could turn the Netherlands from a province of Spain into a territory of France. As either Spanish or French territory, the Netherlands was an equal threat to England's independence, and Elizabeth greatly preferred to have the situation there continue in a state of flux. Almost as much as Philip, but for different reasons, she hated to commit herself by definite actions. She was prepared to fight for her beloved country like a mother in order to achieve the results she wanted. But since she was also an expert in the art of political maneuvering, her weapons were subtle ones: evasions, half-truths, denials. Elizabeth is said to

Catherine de Médicis saw three of her sons in succession crowned king of France. A fourth, Francis, Duke of Alençon (below), she proposed as a match for Queen Elizabeth.

BRIEL

Der herr von Lumei

From the port of Brielle, being besieged by
the Spaniards in the engraving above, the
Sea Beggars inaugurated a fresh Protestant
rebellion in the Netherlands. Sieges were a
feature of the long struggle and were aided
by some of the weapons illustrated here. The
"sausages" of wooden strips at center and
extreme right may have been used to fill in
dikes; the floating fort and the mobile draw-
bridge were useful in a land of waterways.

40

have been the most accomplished liar in Christendom.

In 1572 Elizabeth took an action that seemed straightforward enough but which was to have astonishing results. She ordered the Sea Beggars to stop using English ports as bases, and she forbade her subjects to help them or trade with them in the future. Apparently she was responding to outraged complaints from Spain about the piracy that was making the Channel impossible as a trade route; to the Spaniards her actions heralded a return to a more peaceful relationship.

In fact, this move brought Spain more headaches than ever. The Sea Beggars, deprived of ports from which they could function, launched an attack on the Netherlands coast, captured the important port of Brielle, and established a new headquarters on Dutch soil. It was the signal for a wave of risings. In one town after another, citizens took up arms, threw out the Spanish garrisons and governors, and held the ports for Prince William, who hastened to raise an army and cross the German border to join them. A full-scale war against the tyranny of Spain had begun. The French Huguenots planned to send a large army to support the Protestant rebels, and even Elizabeth dispatched a small group of volunteers.

But the Huguenot army never materialized. In August, 1572, Catherine de Médicis, jealous of the influence that Admiral Coligny, the Huguenot leader, had acquired over her son, abandoned her relationship with the Huguenots

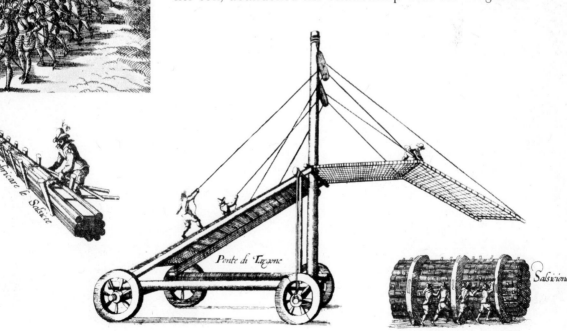

and joined with the rabidly Catholic Duke of Guise in a plot to destroy this threat to her power. The leading Huguenots were all assembled in Paris to celebrate the marriage of the king's sister, Margaret, to Henry of Navarre, the Protestant prince who was the next heir to the throne after the royal brothers. Catherine persuaded Charles that the Huguenots planned to seize the throne, and on the eve of St. Bartholomew's Day, August 23, he gave the order for what became the Massacre of St. Bartholomew. Coligny was murdered, along with thousands of other men, women, and children. For days the streets of Paris and the major provincial cities ran with blood, and the Huguenots who survived abandoned all interest in anything but revenge.

Few Huguenots survived the horrors of the St. Bartholomew massacre; one who did left this scene of the butchery that filled Paris' streets and the Seine (left) with corpses.

The Catholic world rejoiced at the "punishment of the Admiral and his sect." Philip wrote to Catherine that it was the "best and most cheerful news which at present could come to me." Protestants, understandably, were horrified. Elizabeth received the French ambassador at the head of a court all clad in the deepest mourning, and Sir William Cecil, now Lord Burghley, told him that the massacre was the greatest crime since the Crucifixion. William of Orange, who had disbanded his army for lack of Huguenot support, made the final decision to become a Protestant, throw in his lot with the Dutch rebels, and lead them in desperate resistance to the Spaniards.

Once the tumult had died down, however, the ultimate effect of the massacre was to loosen for a while the ties forming between England and France and to bring about new cordiality between England and Spain.

Philip was getting deeper into debt with every year and was finding the Dutch towns more defiant than he expected. He recalled the Duke of Alva, sent a more tolerant governor to replace him, and made friendly overtures to Elizabeth. In return, Elizabeth, eager for peace at almost any price, called her sea dogs to heel and set them to work restoring order in the Channel. Her own traders were beginning to suffer from the privateers' indiscriminate attacks, and like all the Tudors she had built her kingdom on the might of merchants. Trade between England and Spain began to flourish once more, and on the surface things seemed quite friendly.

But the presence of a well-trained Spanish army in the Netherlands, just across the North Sea, was a permanent threat to England. Once the Dutch had been subdued for good, Englishmen knew themselves to be the natural next objective. Elizabeth began to look for enterprises that might strengthen her country and bring in money in some other way than by increasing taxes—a move she hated to make. It was here that Francis Drake awoke her interest.

Drake had been busy in the years since San Juan de Ulua. He had made several visits to the Caribbean and the Isthmus of Panama, some to spy out the land, some to make actual attacks on the property of his "personal" enemy, the king of Spain. From the last of these raids, in 1573, he had returned with a good deal of treasure stolen from the mule trains that brought Peruvian gold and silver across the isthmus to be loaded on the ships of the treasure fleet—rather too much treasure, in fact, for Elizabeth to be altogether pleased with his reappearance at a time when

With Catherine de Médicis looking on, Charles IX stands armed on a balcony of the Louvre during the St. Bartholomew's Day massacre.

she was seeking to mend the breach with King Philip. For four years, therefore, Drake had not been heard from. But he had been busy making plans.

While in Panama, he had climbed a huge tree and had seen, shining in the sun, the vast expanse of the Pacific Ocean, a sight no previous Englishman had laid eyes on. Descending, he fell to his knees and prayed God to give him the chance to sail in an English ship upon that sea. He had not forgotten his prayer.

In 1577, Drake proposed to Sir Francis Walsingham, who had succeeded Lord Burghley as secretary of state, that he be allowed to make the venture. He would sail around South America through the Strait of Magellan and into the Pacific. To the south of the strait was believed to lie a new continent: *Terra Australis Incognita*, the "Unknown Southern Land." He would explore it, prospect for gold, and make friends with its lords with a view to establishing colonies there. There was another, secret, part of the plan: if the opportunity should arise, he would also plunder the king of Spain's wealthy colonies, chiefly Peru and its mines. It seems that Walsingham and the queen gave their consent, on condition that this part of the plan was not revealed in advance. A syndicate of businessmen was formed to raise the capital for ships and men, and the official story was put about that the expedition was going to Egypt.

On November 15, 1577, Drake set out. He had three fighting ships, the largest being the 120-ton *Pelican*. Eighteen months later one of the ships, the *Elizabeth*, struggled into Plymouth. Her captain, John Winter, told of the little fleet's voyage through the Strait of Magellan, complicated by a terrible storm that lasted more than a month. The ships had been separated, and the *Elizabeth* was driven back into the strait. Winter had waited there a month for his admiral before being forced by his frightened crew to return home. Drake and all with him must be dead; no one could have lived in such seas.

But Drake was alive, and busier than he had ever been. After being driven far south into the Antarctic Ocean, he had come to the conclusion that there was no lost continent south of the strait. He had lost his other fighting ship in the storm that parted him from the *Elizabeth*. Inaugurating a fresh stage of his adventure by renaming the little *Pelican*, his sole remaining vessel, the *Golden Hind*, he sailed up the west coast of South America, appearing as if by magic in the Spanish ports. Swooping in on the undefended coast, where no ships but Spanish ones had ever been seen, he

An imaginative Elizabethan depicted the Netherlands as a lean cow from whose back Philip II's spurs draw blood as the Duke of Alva milks her into a pail. William of Orange holds her head so that Elizabeth may offer a handful of hay. The cow thinks poorly of the Duke of Alençon, who pulls her tail.

filled the hold of the *Golden Hind* with treasure from one rich
vessel after another. Then he vanished.

He popped up again off Nicaragua, where he captured
a small ship carrying two pilots bound for the Philippines.
The detailed charts of their route across the Pacific that
Drake took from them were worth more than treasure.
Drake sailed on to the north, seeking the Northwest Passage
that was supposed to link the Atlantic and the Pacific. He
did not find it, and the weather was growing cold, so he
turned south again and landed in a country he called New
Albion to make some repairs to his ship. Before he left he

45

During his round-the-world voyage Drake made frequent stops to repair damage caused by sea worms and weeds. Above, his crew mends a boat on the Brazilian coast. Below, Drake is honored by a chief of the land he called New Albion.

solemnly claimed the land as a territory of Queen Elizabeth's. (Somewhat later it was to be renamed California.) Then he headed west, across the Pacific.

Three months and many adventures later, he came to the Moluccas, or Spice Islands, which were Portuguese territory. Here he made an alliance with the sultan and took on six tons of cloves, which were almost as valuable as gold in a Europe where cooks were always trying to disguise the taste of tainted meat.

Sailing west again, both ship and crew were nearly lost when the *Golden Hind* ran aground on a reef. For twenty hours she hung there while her crew desperately tried to lighten her by throwing much of the cargo overboard. Then the wind changed, and she floated off undamaged.

Two months later Drake was in Java, and by the spring of 1580 he was rounding Africa's Cape of Good Hope into the Atlantic again. Near the end of September, 1580, he came sailing into Plymouth Sound, the first Englishman to circumnavigate the earth. As he passed a fishing boat he leaned over the bulwarks of the *Golden Hind* and shouted, "Is the queen still alive and well?" It was a natural question. He had been away for three years, and in that time everything might have changed.

There had been many changes, in fact, and one of the most important concerned Drake himself. He had become famous; his portrait was in demand all over Europe. *El Draque*—"the Dragon"—the Spaniards called him, and he was said to possess a magic mirror that showed him everything that was happening anywhere in the world. Elizabeth had been deluged with protests from Spain about the deeds of this "master thief," and she had replied with shocked innocence, denying everything, as she always did.

There were other changes too, vital ones. The king of Portugal had died, and King Philip of Spain, his legitimate heir, had taken over the country, adding its vast empire to his own. This meant, of course, that France and England were drawing closer in consequence. The Duke of Alençon, the French king's brother, had just paid a visit to England, and everyone was talking about the possibility that the queen might really marry him.

King Philip had installed a new governor in the Netherlands: Alexander Farnese, Duke of Parma. Under his leadership all the southern provinces had been subdued, although William of Orange and his supporters stubbornly held out in the north. Many Englishmen were insisting that the queen should send more aid to the beleaguered

In 1579 Drake left in New Albion a tablet claiming the country for his queen; he hammered a sixpence into the brass to substantiate it. In 1936 the brass plate at right was picked up near San Francisco. Signed by Drake, and dated 1579, it even has a hole for the sixpence.

Dutch. Louder still were the voices of those of her councilors who saw that war with Spain was inevitable and who wanted her to take action before Philip did.

Money had to be found to help Elizabeth's allies and to prepare for danger. The treasure that Drake brought back was equivalent to twice Elizabeth's entire annual revenue, about fifteen million dollars by modern reckoning. The investors in the voyage received a return much better than 4,000 per cent. Drake's personal share made him an exceedingly rich man. But a huge sum, perhaps as much as half the profits, seems to have dropped quietly into the royal strongboxes. It was enough to make the queen grateful, and enough for her to ignore the Spanish demands that it be returned.

At the queen's orders, Drake brought the *Golden Hind* up the Thames to Deptford and anchored there. On April 4, 1581, Elizabeth came down the river in her royal barge, attended by the Duke of Alençon's special envoy, and went aboard this ship whose name was to go down in history. After a splendid banquet, Elizabeth made Drake kneel before her. The king of Spain, she said, laughing, wanted his head; well, she had a sword with which to cut it off. Then, at her command, the French envoy touched Drake's shoulder with the sword, and he was made a knight.

It was more than a recognition of his achievement in circling the globe; even more than a reward for the Crown's share of the loot. It united France and England in a gesture of defiance against the king of Spain.

48

III

ON A COLLISION COURSE

One evening in 1581 Sir Francis Drake, England's current hero, was invited to dine with some noblemen. At the table one of them asked him if it had really been such a great feat to take a Spanish treasure ship with only eight armed men aboard. Annoyed, the famous captain boasted that he was quite able to make war on the king of Spain himself, if need be. The Earl of Sussex snapped at him for his impudence. Indeed, it sounded more like madness than impudence, for no monarch had ever ruled so much of the earth as King Philip of Spain.

In 1556 the vast possessions of Emperor Charles V had been divided between his brother, Ferdinand, who became Holy Roman Emperor, and his son Philip. The son's primary share was the kingdoms of Castile and Aragon. But he was also Duke of Milan, Naples, and Dijon, Count-Regent of Brussels, lord of the Netherlands, of Sicily, and Franche-Comté, and ruler of most of the New World. Now, with the annexation of Portugal, his empire stretched eastward too, far into the Orient.

Yet Philip's empire seethed with unrest and was threatened by enemies on all sides. The Netherlands was rebellious, Portugal had to be consolidated, and the Spanish territories in America needed better defenses. In France the Duke of Guise and his Holy League of Catholics would continue to fight the Huguenots, led by Henry of Navarre, as long as Philip provided the bank roll. But now that Spain and Portugal were united, Catherine de Médicis and her son Henry III, who had succeeded Charles IX in 1574, would do all they could to prevent any further increase in Philip's power. Their scheme was to propose the

A reserved, artistic, deeply religious man, Philip II (opposite, about 1579) inherited the exhausting duty of ruling half the world. Above, Spain's coat of arms combines castles, for Castile, with the lions of Leon province.

Duke of Alençon not only as a husband for Elizabeth of England but as a leader for the Dutch provinces. In Rome, English Catholic exiles were busy urging upon the pope all kinds of undertakings against England in order to remove Elizabeth from the throne and put Mary Stuart there instead. The pope had reissued a 1570 declaration excommunicating Elizabeth, so her Catholic subjects no longer felt they owed allegiance to her. Jesuit missionary priests were being sent to travel around England in secret, reminding Catholics there that their duty toward the Church meant that they must continue to practice the Catholic faith, and, if necessary, endure persecution for doing so. Philip was constantly being asked for advice and help in arranging this crusade against England, and although he had not felt able to take action while he was so busy with his Portuguese affairs, he was supremely conscious that destiny marked him out as champion of the Catholic Church.

Since 1563 Philip had been building himself a headquarters that was really a retreat among the bare rocks

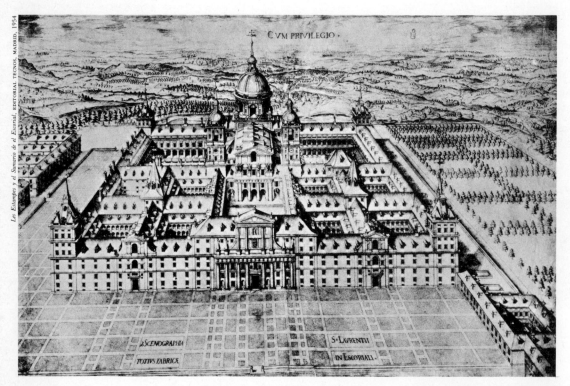

Begun in 1563, the Escorial took twenty-one years to build. The 1587 drawing above shows its gridiron pattern, commemorating St. Lawrence's death by roasting. The library (opposite) holds 30,000 books, 4,000 manuscripts.

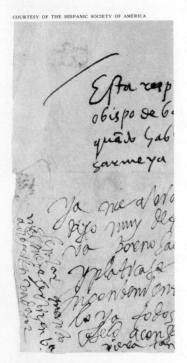

"No secretary in the world uses more paper than His Majesty," one of Philip's advisers complained. Above, the afterthoughts scrawled by the king take up more space than the original neatly written note.

of the Guadarrama Mountains in central Spain. The Escorial was part monastery, part palace, and an ideal place for a man who cherished privacy. There, in a suite of tiny rooms too cramped for courtiers to visit him, and where even his beloved family could not share his life all the time, Philip tried to administer his empire singlehandedly. His father, Emperor Charles, had urged him to be cautious, to trust no one, to listen to advice, but always to make his own decisions. This was the pattern of Philip's life. To his desk came thousands of reports, official documents of all sorts, news, and letters. Although it would have been a taxing job for a dozen officials, Philip sifted through all of it, dictating steadily to his secretaries and making painstaking entries on the specially wide-margined paper.

In the past, he had had help from his family. As he signed his letters *"Yo, el Rey"* for "I, the King," the queen would throw sand from a shaker to dry the ink, and then his two little daughters would take turns carrying the letters over to a table by the window where his secretary would fold and seal them. But since his wife's death in 1580, Philip worked on his own, far into the night, always falling a little further behind with the piles of paper. Religious services were his chief diversion. Leaving his desk, he would pad down the narrow hall, in the soft carpet slippers he wore to ease the pain from his gout, to a slanting window overlooking the monastery chapel, and there in concealment listen to the priests celebrating mass. Quiet, shy, and melancholy, almost always dressed in black, he was once mistaken for a court official by a visitor to the Escorial. Plied with questions about the magnificent collection of pictures that he himself had acquired, Philip answered most kindly and showed the stranger several of the more outstanding exhibits without revealing who he was.

One of the king's most hard-working correspondents was his current ambassador to England, Don Bernardino de Mendoza. It was he who reported Drake's dinnertime boast to the Earl of Sussex. It was undoubtedly also he who in the summer of 1581 gave Philip his first news of England's next move in a campaign of defiance against Spain.

Philip's claim to Portugal was disputed by Don Antonio de Crato, the illegitimate nephew of the late king, who had been seeking help for his cause from both France and England. It occurred to Elizabeth and her advisers that an alliance to aid Don Antonio might be a means of uniting France and England more closely. The Portuguese-owned Azores, those key islands that commanded the trade route

Philip's beloved daughters, Isabella (left) and Catherine, were painted about 1571, at ages five and four. They helped the king with his papers, and when he traveled, he wrote them long chatty letters.

across the Atlantic to the Caribbean, had declared their support for Don Antonio. The English plan was that Drake would go to the chief island of Terceira with a fighting fleet of English and French ships and use the Azores as a base from which to attack Philip's treasure fleets. To avoid embroiling England or France, all would be done in Don Antonio's name and under his flag. With Drake, as his vice-admiral, would go one of England's most experienced captains, Martin Frobisher.

Troubles beset the Portuguese plan. Frobisher, a Yorkshireman, had won fame but not fortune with his explorations beyond Greenland and Labrador in search of the Northwest Passage. He was an ex-privateer, a tough, adventurous man with a violent temper. Drake knew his own

53

ability and was often both high-handed and arrogant. Frobisher resented his success, and the two men struck sparks from each other. Then Drake accused another of the captains of giving information to the Spanish ambassador. Don Antonio demanded a larger fleet. The queen began to worry about the amount of money involved. King Henry of France and Catherine de Médicis refused to join unless Elizabeth committed herself openly. She did not trust them enough to do so. At last the whole venture collapsed.

This fresco depicting the galleys of Spain rowing out to meet Don Antonio's ships (right) at Terceira in 1582 is in the Escorial's great Hall of Battles.

Drake settled down on his Devonshire estates to live like a landed gentleman. He bought manors, served a term as mayor of Plymouth, and busied himself with farming and such shore affairs as laying a conduit to bring fresh drinking water to the city.

Don Antonio took himself off to France, where he succeeded in raising a fleet privately. He found a commander named Philip Strozzi, and in 1582 they sailed for Terceira, hoping to take the islands without English help. Philip, who knew of their plans, sent his Captain General of the Ocean Sea, the Marquis of Santa Cruz, in pursuit.

Santa Cruz was the foremost seaman in Spain. He was the hero of the Battle of Lepanto, the great sea fight in 1571 in which Spain had beaten the Ottoman navy, driving the infidels from the western Mediterranean. His fleet was smaller than Strozzi's, and at first the French had the upper hand. But the wily old marquis got between them and the wind, blasted them with his heavy guns at close range, and captured Strozzi's flagship. Strozzi himself was killed, and Don Antonio fled back to France. King Philip now not only controlled the sea routes between Spain and the West Indies but was the uncontested ruler of Portugal.

Flushed with the enthusiasm of victory and believing that he had conquered English as well as French ships at Terceira, Santa Cruz declared that Philip could be ruler of England too. The admiral proposed keeping his present fleet together as a nucleus around which more ships could be collected. In this way a truly great armada, or fleet, could be massed—a navy of unequaled strength. With a huge army on board, the fleet could sail against England, defeat whatever ships opposed it, land its troops in England, and return the country to Catholicism once more.

Philip found the idea appealing but perhaps too complicated to achieve. Also, he drew back from the thought of open war. Too many other problems were demanding his attention and his money at the moment. He asked Santa Cruz to prepare a plan for him and a detailed estimate of what would be needed so that he could consider the matter of the "Enterprise against England."

Actually, it took several plans and several years before the final estimate appeared in the king's cluttered office in the Escorial. It called for 556 ships and an army of nearly 95,000 men. To feed this gigantic host would require fantastic quantities of food and drink: some 42,000,000 pounds of bacon; 1,800,480 pounds of salt beef; more than 7,000,000 bushels of rice, peas, and beans; 5,000,000 gallons of wine and about half that quantity of water; and such other items as 50,000 strings of garlic for flavoring. The cost of the Enterprise was calculated precisely at 1,526,425,498 maravedis—about sixteen and a half million dollars.

Philip put the plan aside. In being realistic, Santa Cruz was asking for the impossible. The king had almost no existing navy. His troops were tied up in the Netherlands. He had already gone bankrupt twice, and even his enormous wealth was barely enough to pay the interest on his debts. The Enterprise took its place in his files. He had other more pressing concerns, chief of which was the resistance movement in the Netherlands.

The Duke of Parma, who had taken command of the Dutch campaign at the end of 1578, was not content simply to fight battles; he knew the country thoroughly and was able to outmaneuver his opponents. One after another the rebel towns fell before his soldiers, and William of Orange and his followers retreated farther to the north.

In an engraving of a 1582 attempt on the life of William of Orange (above), guards take revenge on the would-be assassin (below, right).

The contest seemed bound to end with a complete Spanish victory. But the courage of the Dutch Protestants won the admiration of Englishmen, and the religious nature of the struggle made it more and more a question of conscience to offer help. English volunteers crossed the Channel to join Prince William. The merchants of London sent a massive financial contribution. Finally, Elizabeth agreed to join in financing an army that would be led by the young Duke of Alençon, her French suitor.

But Alençon failed to get support from France, from England, or from William's supporters. Parma's progress through the Netherlands was irresistible, and Alençon could do nothing to stop it, save make a futile and treacherous attempt to seize Antwerp for himself. In the end he was shipped back to France, where he died in 1584. Elizabeth wept at the tidings. So did Catherine de Médicis, for Alençon had been the last direct heir to the throne, and the man who would now succeed the childless Henry III would be the Protestant Henry of Navarre. The Duke of Guise and his Holy League took a solemn vow never to recognize a Protestant king; they redoubled their efforts to stamp out the Huguenots and Henry along with them.

Then, a month after Alençon's death, another occurred to make Elizabeth, and all the Protestant world, grieve.

For years Philip had offered a reward to the person who would assassinate William of Orange, a man Catholics considered a dangerous criminal. Four attempts on William's life were made between 1582 and 1584. Finally, in July, 1584, a young fanatic, hiding behind a pillar in William's house in Delft, shot the prince through the heart.

The loss of the revered Dutch leader shook the whole land, but it did not put an end to the revolt. Parma took city after city: Brussels and Ghent in 1584, Antwerp, after a long siege, in 1585. Still the Dutch fought on, offering the sovereignty of their little group of states to Elizabeth, and when she refused, banding together under the banner of William's young son, Maurice.

The year 1585 was to be the point at which a long cold war turned into a hot one. It was becoming apparent to Philip and to the Duke of Parma that the Netherlands would never be subdued as long as Dutch sea power and English assistance continued unchecked. In order to destroy both of these, England had to be invaded.

As for England, feeling at William's assassination ran so high that Elizabeth was finally forced into direct action on her own. Her councilors, if not she herself, feared a simi-

A 1630 version of Mendoza's expulsion from England shows the Spanish ambassador sneaking off with lists of vital information.

lar attempt on her life. One had been planned, in 1583, by the Duke of Guise, Mary Stuart, and Mendoza, with or without King Philip's direct consent. It was exposed, Mendoza dismissed, and Mary placed under closer guard. But the danger of another plot was always present. Accordingly, Elizabeth began negotiating with the Dutch about sending a force of soldiers to help the Netherlands.

While she was doing so, Philip took a decisive step himself. He ordered his port commanders to seize all shipping found on his coasts, including that of the Netherlands, England, "and other provinces that are in rebellion against me." His ports just happened at the same time to contain an unusual number of English ships. They had sailed, under safe conduct from the king, to bring wheat for sale to relieve a famine in Spain. All but one of the English ships were seized as soon as they entered port; that one, the *Primrose*, escaped and carried back word of what had happened.

It was a piece of treachery that reminded everyone of San Juan de Ulua, and England was in an uproar. Elizabeth summoned Sir Francis Drake, who was fitting out an expedition to the Moluccas, and gave him fresh instructions. He was to sail to Spain, and on her behalf demand the release of the captured vessels and their crews.

In haste he gathered twenty-one ships and eight pinnaces, a formidable fleet, with some two thousand soldiers and sailors to man it. The queen provided two ships and a royal commission so that Drake might fly her flag. All the rest were contributed by shareholders, including Drake himself, since even a voyage like this was also a business venture. Merchants risked their ships and men, and they liked to be able to show some profit when the fighting was over. Drake's flagship, the *Bonaventure*, was a royal galleon of 600 tons; Frobisher was his vice-admiral; and some of England's most distinguished families provided officers who were eager to fight on her behalf. On September 14 the avenging flotilla set sail.

Drake had left England in such a hurry that his water casks were half empty. Picking up a few small prizes on the way, he sailed to the port of Vigo, on the northern coast of

On his way to the Caribbean in 1585, Drake stopped at the Cape Verde Islands, where he hoped to hold the town of Santiago for ransom. In this bird's-eye view, his ships command the bay while his soldiers (right), led by drummers, advance upon the town, whose defenders are fleeing to safety (left). Angered at finding no treasure, Drake burned Santiago to the ground.

This detail from a chart illustrating a sixteenth-century account of Drake's exploits in the Caribbean adds a fanciful sea monster to an otherwise realistic picture of his successful assault on Cartagena.

Spain. There he put in to take on supplies and water and learned that the arrest had already been lifted. He freed some English prisoners, helped himself to 6,000 ducats' worth of plunder from the town, and disappeared. King Philip's council fumed at such an insult, but they were helpless, for there were no ships ready to stop *el Draque*, and in any case no one knew where he had gone.

He had in fact sailed westward to the Caribbean. Without warning, on the last day of December, he arrived off Santo Domingo, the capital of Hispaniola. He landed troops, bombarded the town with his ships' guns, and by the dawn of New Year's Day the place had surrendered to him. To his disappointment he found no great treasure there and had to make do with a ransom of 25,000 ducats.

Drake could not hold Santo Domingo because fever had decimated his troops and he had not enough men. He went on to Cartagena, headquarters of trade along the Spanish Main and a city whose defenses he knew. Once again speed and surprise won the day. While the ships bombarded the town, the infantry worked its way silently up under the walls and then charged them. There was a short, hot fight, and the English swept right into the city and took it. Once again Drake had to accept a ransom, this time of 100,000 ducats, instead of the treasure he had hoped to find.

In July, 1586, he came home to Plymouth again. Financially the voyage had not been the success he had hoped, for he had also planned—and failed—to capture a treasure fleet. But he had shown Spain something of England's strength at sea by taking and holding for ransom the two greatest Spanish cities in the Caribbean. As Secretary of State Walsingham wrote to the Earl of Leicester, "The enterprise of Sir Francis Drake layeth open the present weakness of the king of Spain, for of late he hath solicited the pope and the dukes of Florence and Savoy for a loan of 500,000 crowns but cannot obtain neither the whole nor part of the said sum." Wise old Burghley, the queen's most trusted adviser, summed the situation up concisely: "Truly, Sir Francis Drake is a fearful man to the king of Spain."

Meanwhile, English intervention in the Netherlands had been less successful. Elizabeth had dispatched six thousand men, just too late to raise the siege of Antwerp, which fell in August, 1585. As their leader she had chosen Robert Dudley, Earl of Leicester.

It was not a good choice. Leicester was the queen's favorite and a brave man, but he was a mediocre military commander who displayed genius only in his ability to antagonize those who should have been his friends. Recognizing that the Dutch provinces desperately needed a strong unifying force, he accepted from them the title of Governor-General. Elizabeth was so furious that she planned to disgrace Leicester publicly. "Jesus!" she wrote to one man who tried to tell her this would be unwise, "what availeth wit when it fails the owner at greatest need? Do that you are bidden and leave your considerations to your own affairs."

Leicester finally won the queen around by offering to return home to work in her stables and "rub her horses' heels." Although she forgave him, his new position was the ruin of English hopes. Rapidly bogging down in administrative duties, Leicester found little time to spare for his army. His officers, inexperienced, and offended by his haughty manner, had trouble controlling their men, who were poorly paid and short of food. They fought well when pressed but won more fame as thieves and plunderers.

In August, 1586, before the town of Zutphen, five hundred heavily armed English horsemen rode gallantly against

Leicester (above) was too late to save Antwerp, which fell despite an attack by Dutch fireships on Parma's bridge of boats (below).

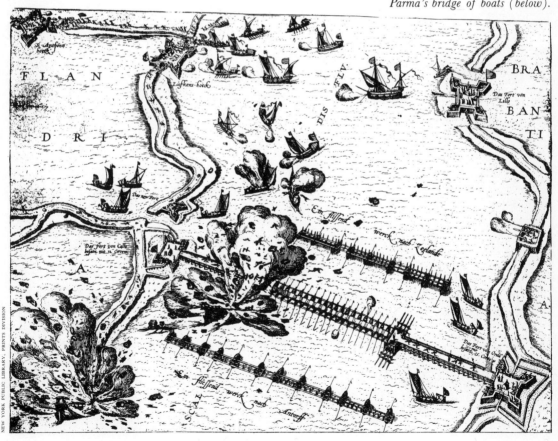

61

nearly ten times their number of Spanish troops. They smashed the Spanish cavalry but were forced to retreat before the infantry, which stood fast behind its long pikes. During the heavy fighting, young Sir Philip Sidney, renowned as a poet and philosopher and the pride of Elizabeth's court, received his death wound. As he lay on the battlefield he refused a drink of water, pointing instead to a wounded soldier and saying, "Give it to him, his need is greater than mine." It was the one heroic gesture to emerge from a frustrating war.

Zutphen marked the end of significant English intervention in the Netherlands. Leicester left for home at the end of the year. With astonishing lack of foresight, he left his two main strongpoints under the command of known Catholics. Elizabeth was disgusted at having spent £126,000, half of her annual income, to so little purpose. The English army had indeed kept Parma from taking the whole of the Netherlands and had disrupted his timetable, but nothing more had been accomplished. Parma dug in for the winter, negotiated with the two English Catholic captains,

From forts around Zutphen (below) the English fought a series of engagements with Parma. Their chief casualty, Philip Sidney, was later given a state funeral (above).

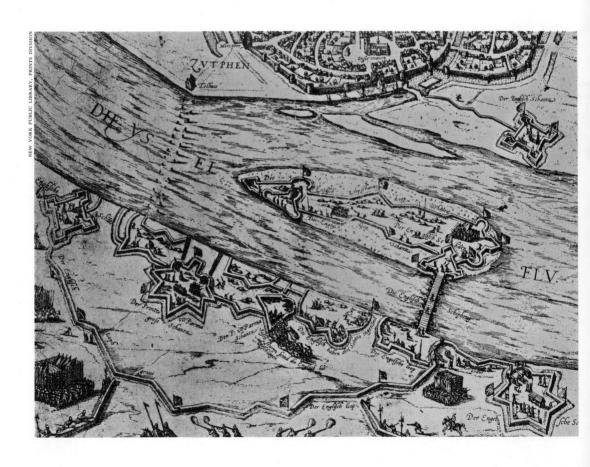

and was able shortly to write King Philip that their fortresses had surrendered to him without a blow being struck.

In Spain, Philip felt new pressure for war against England. The Marquis of Santa Cruz laid on the king's desk a new and up-to-date estimate for the Enterprise. Just across the Channel from the English ports lay the victorious armies of the Duke of Parma—why could they not be used against England herself? The original plans Santa Cruz had prepared called for transporting a huge army all the way from Spain. Here was one ready at hand, only needing to be ferried quickly and safely across the Channel. Parma himself suggested that his men could do the job in flat-bottomed boats, without the help of Santa Cruz and his fleet.

Still Philip hesitated, weighing all the chances. "He fears war," wrote an exiled English Catholic in Rome, "as a burned child dreads the fire."

At this point, something happened that was to bring everything to a head. Indeed, it had been arranged to do so.

After the 1583 plot against Elizabeth's life, Mary Queen of Scots had been placed in strict confinement, with her every move closely watched. Sir Francis Walsingham, who maintained a network of spies rivaling Philip's own, knew she would try to reopen a secret correspondence from her new prison. He therefore set up a double agent to give her a means of doing so. The local brewer was prepared to carry letters in and out in the bung of a beer barrel—only Walsingham's men copied the correspondence before sending it along. Unaware of the trap, Mary began to use the secret line; before long, Walsingham's planning paid off.

Anthony Babington, a young Derbyshire gentleman, was plotting, with the help of a priest named Ballard and five others, to raise a rebellion among the English Catholics and make Mary queen. A letter from Babington to Mary in July, 1586, outlined the whole plan. Parma would land Spanish troops, Babington would deliver Mary from prison, and the plotters would "dispatch the usurping competitor" as Elizabeth walked in her garden. No action could be taken, however, until Mary's reply came through the mail. When it did, it implicated her completely.

A roar went up for revenge against all who were involved in the conspiracy. Ever since Mary's first intrigue against her cousin in 1571, Elizabeth's ministers had demanded Mary's death, and they did so now in terms Elizabeth could not refuse.

The queen still wavered. It was a dangerous precedent to put another monarch to death—officially. How would Mary's son, James VI, now reigning as king of Scotland, consider the execution of his mother? What would be the effect on the king of Spain? And what would France do?

Most of all, Elizabeth feared to take so completely final a step. The French envoy more or less agreed with her: "I tell you, Madame," he said, "that instead of arresting the invasion . . . you will only precipitate it. Hitherto, the Queen of Scots has been the target which has caught the

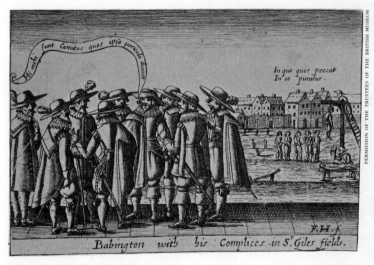

Babington with his Complices in St Giles fields.

Queen Elizabeth (opposite), who counted her people's love "the chief glory of my crown," always went about unguarded, even in the months it took Sir Francis Walsingham (above left) to gather evidence that Babington and his friends (above right) planned to murder her and make Mary Stuart queen.

couingfinne van fchoflan

In this contemporary Dutch water color, Mary Queen of Scots, a crucifix in her hands, is beheaded. Her ladies in waiting were allowed to witness her death provided they did not weep, but as can be seen, they failed to keep their promise.

arrows that have been aimed at your person. She is a stone that you hold in your hand. Fling it at your enemy and it is gone; you can threaten with it no more."

Mary was brought to trial on October 14, 1586, and the court urged that she be sentenced to death. But Elizabeth would not put her name to the death warrant. She put the matter off again and again, although her chief advisers, Walsingham and Burghley, kept pressing her to sign.

Finally, on February 10, 1587, she did so—and the next day asked for the warrant back again. But her secretary, Mr. William Davison, had given it immediately to the Lord Chancellor, who had put the queen's seal on it. At a special meeting of the Privy Council, held without her knowledge, Burghley took the awesome responsibility of making up Elizabeth's mind for her—and sent the warrant on its way.

A messenger set out on Saturday, February 14, to deliver the warrant to the earls of Shrewsbury and Kent, who were at Fotheringay Castle where Mary was a prisoner. On Sunday evening he arrived and handed the document to the earls. They read it and went to tell Mary to prepare for death. On the morning of Wednesday, February 18, she was brought into the great hall of the castle. Determined to die like a martyr for her faith, she knelt with dignity before the block, and a few moments later the tragic life of Mary Queen of Scots was ended. But the mischief had only begun.

When the news was brought to Elizabeth, one onlooker reported that she "fell into such deep grief of mind . . . as the like had never been seen." According to another, she received the news without apparently turning a hair. Both reports may well have been true. Elizabeth knew how to act a part better than any other woman, and only she knew which reaction was the real one.

Although she had not been averse to having the deed done in some way that would not throw the blame on her, now that the legal execution was performed she flew into one of her royal rages. Davison was sent to the Tower of London; Burghley was ordered out of her presence. (The latter was too invaluable not to be pardoned within a couple of months, but although Davison was eventually released from the Tower, his career was finished.) Some of Elizabeth's anger may have been genuine; some may have been to impress the king of Spain. If so, it was a waste of time, for the French envoy in a way had been right: although the king of Spain had long since decided to invade England, Mary's death removed the last reason for delay.

The danger of making England a territory of France was over. In her will, Mary Stuart had bequeathed England to King Philip. The whole Catholic world now looked to him to avenge her death. And it was clear, after the insult of Drake's raids on Santo Domingo and Cartagena, that Elizabeth meant war as much as he did.

On March 31, 1587, a little more than a month after Mary's execution, a spate of letters began pouring out of the king's office in the Escorial. Some went to Rome, telling the English Catholic exiles there to prepare themselves and asking the Spanish emissary to make another try for a papal loan, for Philip was still short of money. One went to his agent in France, another to Parma in the Netherlands. But the most important was the letter sent to the Marquis of Santa Cruz. It ordered him to have the Enterprise against England ready to sail before summer began.

Lord Burghley (above) was a wise administrator of England's meager funds. Philip of Spain, also short of money, had to ask the pope for a loan. A Protestant playing card satirizes the situation by presenting the pope as the knave of hearts.

IV

SINGEING THE KING
OF SPAIN'S BEARD

By early 1587 King Philip had begun to look upon his Enterprise as a combined operation by land and sea. In the Netherlands, he had the best general in all Europe, the Duke of Parma, and his Spanish infantrymen had never been beaten in a pitched battle. If the king could raise a fleet of ships strong enough to clear the Channel of all intruders, Parma's men would be able to cross in small boats from the Netherlands ports to the English coast. There, they would land and take the stubbornly Protestant island by storm.

Parma had reservations about linking up with the fleet without an adequate deepwater harbor in which to do it. Nevertheless, he sent Philip a letter saying he was ready.

The only sour note was that struck by old Santa Cruz. A professional sailor, he knew the difficulty of sailing up the Channel, fighting off English opposition all the way, and meeting Parma at precisely the right moment to convoy him to England. For such a ticklish mission he needed as many ships as he could get, at least 50 galleons, 100 "greatships," 40 galleys, and nearly 200 other craft to transport stores and run errands. Busy as he had been in assembling ships and stores from the vast resources of the Spanish empire, he still had only a fraction of that force.

The galleon, the basic fighting ship of the day, was a two- or three-decker, usually with three masts, and carried a heavy armament of guns. It was longer in proportion to

Sixteenth-century mariners had to be able to read charts, note landfalls, sound depths, and watch weather, in addition to sailing their ships. Opposite, the title page of a 1588 navigational handbook shows seamen taking soundings amid several contemporary measuring devices. The compass rose above, from a chart made the same year, shows a southwest wind blowing.

its width than were the greatships, which were really armed merchantmen, and thus was a faster sailer. At bow and stern rose wooden "castles." These were relics of the Middle Ages, when fighting at sea was carried on like a land fight, with ships grappling each other and soldiers attacking out of what were really floating forts. Both forecastle and sterncastle bristled with small guns that could be turned down upon enemy boarders in the waist. Ranged along the decks and protected by high wooden sides were the heavy cannons for use against enemy ships. These warships had high sloping sides, which were hard for boarders to climb, and their length and weight enabled them to carry great numbers of guns.

The Spanish method of sea fighting was to pound an enemy ship at close range with heavy artillery, then move in closer still, and with smaller guns kill as many men on deck as possible in preparation for grappling and boarding. Sailors were a necessary but inferior group who maneuvered the vessels; the real work was done by soldiers, led by noble officers. To the Spaniards, ships were platforms on which to use pikes and swords, and guns only opened the way for more glorious hand-to-hand combat.

Santa Cruz also favored the use of galleys, which were traditional with the Spaniards. A massive force of galleys had given him his stunning victory at Lepanto. Long and narrow, they were driven by banks of oars, rowed by slaves, and thus had no need to rely on the wind. They had long iron beaks at their prows, and carried guns only in bow or stern, since their waists were full of rowers. The galleys' technique was to dart in swiftly at close quarters while clumsier enemies were trying to maneuver into position and ram them with their sharp beaks.

They had a serious deficiency, however, apart from needing a large complement of slaves to row them and being able to carry only a minimum of artillery. They had been developed for use in the Mediterranean, and their slimness and lightness made them poor vessels for the rough Atlantic.

Recognizing this, the Spaniards had recently been developing a new kind of ship, called a galleass, which was supposed to combine the good points of both galleon and galley. Heavier, deeper, and wider than a galley, but lighter than a galleon, it used both sails and oars as a means of maneuvering, and on a roofed-in deck above the rowers, it carried an impressive broadside of guns.

England, whose seamen were constantly facing Atlantic

Elizabethan warships could pack 400 men between decks barely six feet high. Gravel ballast and a storage area filled the hold. On the decks above, men lived alongside the guns, on rations of one pound of biscuit and one gallon of sour beer a day, and used the "head," or beakhead, in the prow as a privy. The primitive galley (right) has one huge cooking pot. Astern (left) are ornately paneled quarters for the officers.

storms, had little use for galleys. Her shipwrights too had been concentrating on a new design, but their aim was to make sailing ships more maneuverable. This task was primarily the achievement of John Hawkins.

In 1577, Hawkins had taken his father-in-law's place as Treasurer of the Navy. "I shall pluck a thorn out of my foot and put it into yours," the older man warned him, and this turned out to be true. The navy Henry VIII had built up so painstakingly had been neglected by his children. Elizabeth had tried to put it into shape without spending much money, and the result of her economies was a poor and corrupt administration and a fleet made up mainly of overage, rotten, and useless ships.

Hawkins made a complete investigation and then set out to correct the mess he had found. He pleased the queen by proposing ways in which money could be saved by eliminating inefficiency. By degrees he was able to reform many of the worst abuses, such as the overcrowding of ships and the low rate of pay for seamen. As a result, when their conditions were improved, better sailors were attracted into the fleet. But the new treasurer realized that success at sea ultimately depended on building faster and more seaworthy vessels.

Like other experienced English sea captains, Hawkins knew that size alone meant nothing. As Sir Walter Raleigh put it, "The greatest ships are the least serviceable. . . . A

The 1571 Battle of Lepanto was fought, as the Spaniards thought sea engagements should be, hand to hand. Carrying the pope's blessing, a combined Italian-Spanish fleet of 300 ships and 80,000 men clashed head on with an equally powerful

mass of Turkish galleys near Greece's Gulf of Corinth. The Christian commander, King Philip's half brother, told his men to hold their fire "until near enough to be splashed with the blood of an enemy" and after a four-hour-long struggle, the infidels fled.

73

ship of 600 tons will carry as good ordnance as a ship of 1,200 tons; and though the greater have double her number, the lesser will turn her broadsides twice before the greater can wind once." The fault in the traditional design was that it not only made ships sluggish in turning or sailing against the wind but made them top-heavy and liable to tip over. The strain of carrying the heavy castles on a ship's frame was so great that such vessels leaked badly in heavy weather.

As Her Majesty's galleons came in for refitting, Hawkins had the high forecastles knocked off and the sterncastles cut down. And when new ships were built, they were made longer than usual and narrower in the beam. The result was a low-bowed, slender ship that could carry more sails and hence could sail closer to the wind and maneuver faster than any comparable vessel.

Hawkins concentrated too on greatships—heavily armed versions of the merchant vessels that he and his fellow sea captains had found so reliable. They were smaller than galleons but nimbler, and when their deep waists had been planked over to make another deck, they carried enough guns for a deadly broadside.

Hawkins did not accomplish his work without making enemies among those whose inefficiency or personal greed he exposed. One such enemy was Sir William Wynter, the queen's Master of Naval Ordnance. But in spite of their differences, Wynter agreed with Hawkins on one important point: the use of guns in sea fights.

Both Wynter and Hawkins were convinced that it was far better to be able to hammer an enemy at a distance than to have to come to grips with him. English ships were sailed by expert and independent seamen. Drake had established the principle that "the gentlemen must hale and draw with the mariners"; and crews and captains worked together with mutual respect. Swift ships and efficient sailors aboard them could make long-range guns most effective.

Under Wynter's direction there was a change in ordnance. The very heavy, short-range cannons firing a fifty-pound ball, such as the Spaniards favored, were almost completely replaced by demicannons, which fired a thirty-pound ball, and by culverins and demiculverins. Culverins were longer barreled than cannons, and so although their round shot weighed less—about seventeen and nine pounds respectively—their range was considerably longer. The culverin, for instance, could hurl a shot about 700 yards

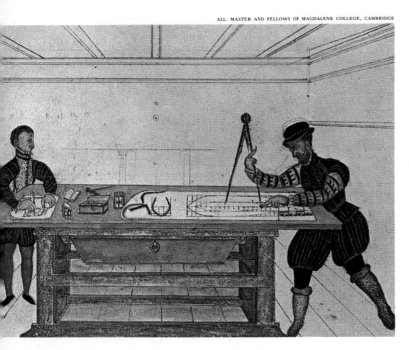

Paintings by master shipwright Matthew Baker show Hawkins' revolutionary design taking shape, first on his drawing board, then as a curving hull is built (right). Below, the completed ship appears alongside its inspiration: a fish.

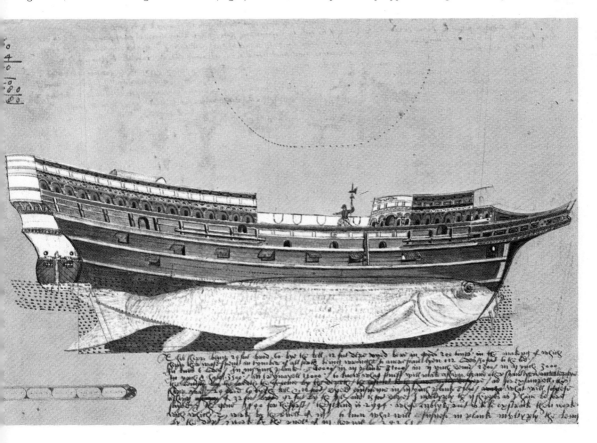

This drum, inscribed with Drake's crest, is the most famous relic of the Armada period. On his death-bed, Drake is said to have vowed to return if drumbeats sounded on it warned of danger to England.

to the demicannon's 500. The increase in range was to change the style of the battles to come.

By the beginning of 1587 the queen's fleet was ready for action, and in the opinion of all its officers it was the best and strongest in the world. Hawkins had done his work well. All that was lacking now was the queen's permission to take it to sea. Reports came in constantly of ships massing in Cadiz and Lisbon, of preparations going on all over Spain. But Elizabeth, as usual, was short of money and eager to continue the uneasy peace a little longer. She hesitated to give a command that would mean large expenditures on mobilizing the fleet and could jeopardize the delicate negotiations she was now carrying on with Parma, as Philip's representative, for a truce in the Netherlands.

But when Walsingham's spies reported that Philip was in earnest and planned an invasion by midsummer, Elizabeth began to listen to the clamorings of her captains, and particularly to Sir Francis Drake. Drake's plan was ready, and its boldness was typical of him. He would gather a private fleet and raid Spanish shipping either at sea or in its own harbors. He could thus see—and, with luck, delay— whatever was afoot and, incidentally, bring back something for Her Majesty's treasury and his own coffers.

A privately financed venture would not be too expensive and could be disowned if it turned out badly. If it was successful in delaying the Spanish preparations even a little, England could use the time valuably. So the queen gave Drake six ships, four of them galleons, with the 550-ton *Elizabeth Bonaventure* as his flagship. The Lord Admiral of England, Lord Howard of Effingham, sent a ship and a pinnace. Drake himself fitted out four ships, and various London merchants contributed enough vessels to bring the total up to twenty-three.

On March 25 Drake received his instructions. Broad enough to satisfy even his fiery soul, they ordered him "to impeach the joining together of the king of Spain's fleets out of their several ports, to keep victuals from them, to follow them in case they should come forward toward England or Ireland, and to cut off as many of them as he could and impeach their landing; as also to set upon such as should either come out of the West or East Indies into Spain or go out of Spain thither." He was even allowed to "distress their ships within their havens."

Drake, who knew well how his queen could change her mind, hastened down to Plymouth and began loading supplies and men as fast as he could. On April 11 the London

FRANCISCVS DRAECK NOBILISSIMVS EQVES ANGLIÆ AN° ÆT SVE 43

Habes Lector candide fortiß. ac inuictiß Ducis Draeck ad Vinam Jmaginem qui toto terrarum orbe, duorum annorum, et mensium decem spatio, Zephiris fauentibus circumducto, Angliam sedes proprias, 4. Cal Octobr. anno á partu Virginis 1580 reuisit cum antea portu soluißet Jd. Decem: anni. 1577.

*This 1583 engraving gave admirers of the man who had circled the globe—
and returned—a portrait "done from life" of Francis Drake at forty-three.*

ships joined him, and the next morning, without waiting to take on the last of his gear, Drake put to sea. He was only just in time. The queen's messenger was already on his way with more cautious instructions. "You shall forbear," the new orders said, "to enter forcibly into any of the said king's ports or havens; or to offer any violence to any of his towns, or shipping within harboring, or to do any act of hostility upon the land." The messenger set out after Drake in a pinnace belonging to Hawkins, but—unaccountably—he failed to catch up with him.

On his first day out, Drake met two English warships, which joined his fleet, raising his strength to twenty-five. A few days later, a severe storm scattered them, and they were not reunited until April 26, when they met, as arranged, off the coast of Portugal. There Drake intercepted two merchantmen, northward bound from Cadiz, who told him that a great number of craft had gathered at that port to take on guns and stores before joining the Marquis of Santa Cruz at Lisbon.

Drake at once set sail for Cadiz. On April 29 he called a council of war on board his flagship. He had one thing in common with his adversary, the king of Spain, which was

At left, bearing the queen's official seal, is Drake's commission as commander of the fleet that sailed to Spain in 1587. At right, the minute attention to detail in Vice-Admiral Borough's chart of Cadiz reveals his own character as well as Drake's activities there.

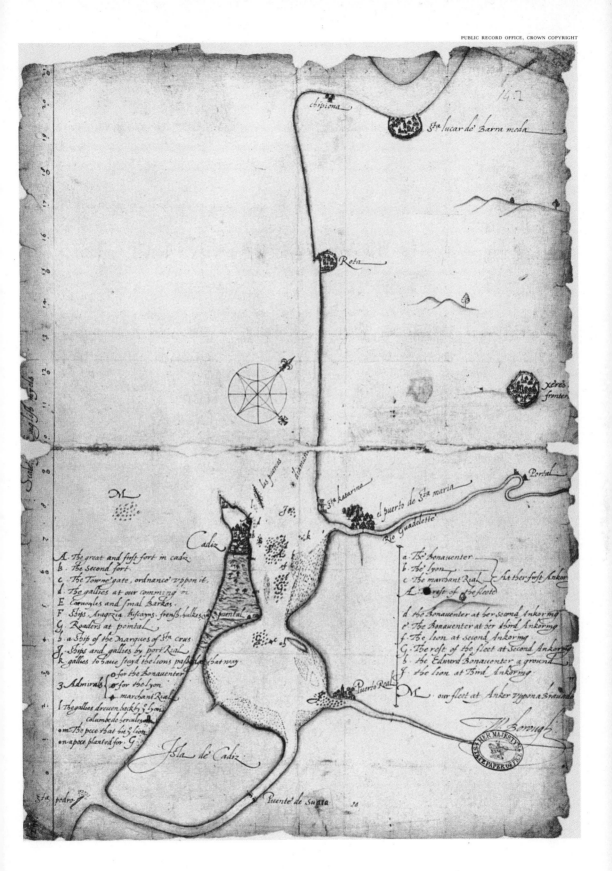

that he asked everyone for his opinion, and after listening to it, did exactly as he pleased. In this case, he announced to his officers that he intended to storm Cadiz that very afternoon, and then he dismissed them. His vice-admiral, William Borough, a veteran of many years at sea and a member of the Navy Board, was shocked by this high-handed procedure. He felt that greater caution ought to be used for such an attempt. Caution, however, was a word unknown to Drake.

The town of Cadiz stood on the summit of a steep cliff at the end of an arm of land some five miles long. This arm, curving out to the northwest, embraced a wide harbor —actually two separate harbors, an outer and an inner one, joined by a narrow channel of water about half a mile wide. Shoals and rocks protected the main entrance, and there were batteries of guns at the tip of the promontory and also commanding the harbor mouth. To William Borough, a headlong attack on such a strong position was a violation of all the rules. Drake, however, delighted in breaking rules. He sailed right in, his fleet in line behind him, with orders to follow and do as he did.

Before them crowded the masts and rigging of nearly sixty vessels. There were hulks, or storeships, being loaded or already full of supplies, and merchantmen of all sorts and sizes from small caravels to a 700-ton, forty-gun Geno-ese greatship waiting to return to Italy. Nearer the inner gun battery was a mass of tiny craft: pinnaces, coasting barks, and fishing boats. There were also some eight or nine galleys, the watchdogs of the port.

As the English sailed in, two of the galleys shot out to question them. They got their answer before they could ask for it: banners broke from the rigging of the *Elizabeth Bona-venture*, trumpets and drums blared, and her guns opened fire. The galleys scurried back to safety.

Panic broke out in the harbor. Most of the smaller boats cut their anchor cables; those light enough slipped over the shallows into the inner harbor. Many of the larger ships, however, were foreign ones that Philip had pressed into service for his Armada, and they had been stripped of their sails so that they could not desert. As they drifted help-lessly, the galleys rowed out to defend them. They ad-vanced in a line abreast, their sharp rams cutting the water, their oars flashing rhythmically. It was a gallant gesture, but a hopeless one. As Drake's four big warships sailed in at the head of his column each one turned, fired a broad-side, and swung away. Their guns outranged the small, light weapons of the galleys, knocking the flimsy bulwarks to bits and stretching men wounded and dying on the rowers' benches. In the face of that deadly barrage, the galleys had to draw off. One was driven on shore in flames, and the rest took refuge in St. Mary's Port, across the bay to the northeast.

The English dropped anchor and began sorting out their prizes. They burned some ships, and put crews aboard those they wished to capture. The big Genoese merchantman opened fire, and Drake's ships wheeled in and smashed her to pieces with one broadside after another. She sank at once, and the English mourned the loss of those forty beautiful brass cannons that they might otherwise have seized. The town battery tried a few salvos, but their guns had been meant to stop an assault up the beaches to the town, not to shoot halfway across the harbor. Two of the galleys came nosing out of St. Mary's Port and fired their bow guns; they succeeded in recapturing a Portuguese caravel that Drake's men had taken, but aside from this, did no damage.

The night passed in the light of the flames of burning ships, with the English working energetically to transfer their loot to their own holds. After dawn, Drake moved his flag to the *Merchant Royal*, one of the London ships, which was somewhat smaller than the *Elizabeth Bonaventure*. In this, and followed by a flotilla of his small pinnaces and ships' boats, he sailed through the entrance to the inner harbor. There, a magnificent galleon, the property of Santa Cruz himself, was anchored, waiting to take on her guns. Drake led his men in an attack, boarded her, looted her, and left her blazing.

At midday he ordered his ships to their positions and prepared to depart. For the first time he was out of luck. The wind died, leaving him becalmed among his foes.

The galleys began creeping out again. Without wind the Englishmen would surely be sitting ducks, unable to maneuver. Now was the time for the rams. But Drake sent out small boats to haul on the bow cables of his ships, turning them through an arc so that he could continue to fire his broadsides. The galleys quickly scuttled back to shelter.

Then the Spaniards began setting fire to the cargoes of their smaller boats, to use them as fireships against the intruders. As they drifted toward the English ships the men went out in pinnaces and fended them off with long poles. "We were not a little troubled to defend us from their terrible fire," wrote one, "which nevertheless was a pleasant

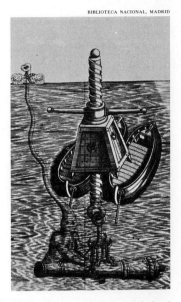

Taken from a 1613 Spanish book on artillery, this illustration shows an early frogman attaching a cable from a floating winch to a sunken cannon in an effort to salvage it.

Cadiz in 1582 was a peaceful port, with fishing boats filling the harbor (right) where Drake made such havoc five years later. Peasants dance on the cliffs while others below draw in nets full of tunny.

sight for us to behold, because we were thereby eased of a great labor . . . in discharging the victuals and other provisions of the enemy." At two in the morning, a land breeze sprang up. Drake ordered all sail set and glided out of a harbor brilliantly lit by burning ships.

He had destroyed between twenty-four (by the Spanish account) and thirty-seven (by his own reckoning) of the Spanish vessels. He had cost the king of Spain nearly 200,000 ducats in losses and had virtually wiped out the Cadiz section of the Armada. He had reprovisioned his own fleet at Spain's expense and had taken six ships full of supplies. But he was not yet finished with his enemy.

While in Cadiz he had learned a good deal that was of interest to him. In Lisbon, Santa Cruz was fitting out the Portuguese galleons of the royal navy and awaiting the arrival of greatships from the Levant fleet and galleasses from Italy, all of them laden with men and supplies for the Enterprise against England. Somewhere in the Atlantic the treasure fleet was homing from the West Indies. And somewhere off Cape St. Vincent, at the southern tip of Portugal, one of Spain's best commanders, Don Juan Martinez de Recalde, was at sea with half a dozen ships, waiting to cover the return of the treasure fleet. The English had intercepted a dispatch from the king ordering Recalde to return to Lisbon and join Santa Cruz.

It seemed to Drake that his best move after leaving

CADIZ, olim Gades, eiusdem no: minis Insulæ oppidum nobile, por: tu maris Herculeo freto, temploque memoratum.

Cadiz would be to go to Cape St. Vincent, surprise Recalde's small squadron, and destroy it. This would deprive Spain of good ships and one of her best captains, while the treasure fleet would be left without additional protection.

Accordingly, he made a dash for Cape St. Vincent but found Recalde gone; he had heard of Drake's activities and had made straight for Lisbon. Something else, however, offered itself. Cape St. Vincent was a strategic point, for it was the most frequently used stopping point for water and shelter on the Atlantic coast. It was guarded by a fortified monastery, with an auxiliary fort on the cliffs, and by Sagres Castle on the other side of a small bay. Drake saw that from this station he could indeed "impeach the joining together of the king of Spain's fleets," and he decided to take it.

At this, Vice-Admiral Borough was thoroughly upset. He drew up a long letter protesting against Drake's behavior. There had been no proper councils, he complained, and the whole campaign thus far had been managed in a very slapdash manner and without respect for other officers. Drake's answer was to deprive Borough of his command and confine him to his cabin under close arrest. He then proceeded with his plan to take the cape.

His first attempt was turned back. The next day he led his men up the steep cliffs to attack a small fort. This was taken quickly, and the company climbed on to Sagres

Details from a contemporary engraving show the sea's influence on life in southwestern Spain. Above, ships take wine barrels on board; below, a fort's cannons warn unfamiliar vessels away from a harbor.

Castle, above it. A two-hour-long fight ended in the surrender of the castle and that of the monastery and its fort as well. Drake razed them all and toppled their guns over the cliff. It would be a long time before Spain could properly defend this important spot.

Drake was now master of the whole area. He sank fifty boats in the tunny-fishing grounds around the cape, boats that should have supplied some of the mountain of salt fish needed for the Armada. He destroyed another fifty vessels carrying cargoes of barrel hoops and staves: the Armada would go short of both food and water without seasoned barrels to carry supplies. Then Drake sailed for Lisbon and anchored in Cascaes Bay. Beyond were the stone walls of St. Julian's Tower, which was Santa Cruz' headquarters, and the battlements of sturdy forts from which jutted the snouts of heavy cannons. In the port were nearly thirty warships and seven galleys. Most of the galleons and greatships had as yet no sails, guns, or crews. As for the galleys, they dared not face Drake's broadsides. The news from Cadiz had traveled fast.

However, if they could not come out, neither could Drake go in after them. The harbor guns were too strong for him, and he had no pilots to negotiate the tricky passage up the Tagus River. He sent insults and challenges in to Santa Cruz and chased every small boat that came in sight. The marquis, with no ships to oppose Drake's force, sat in St. Julian's Tower and bided his time.

Drake returned to Cape St. Vincent, demonstrating how useful it was to have this comfortable way station. Now he could let his men take some much-needed rest, change his ballast, and clean out his ships. He wrote to Walsingham of what he had done, saying that he had singed the king of Spain's beard. "God make us all thankful again and again that we have, though it be little, made a beginning on the coast of Spain," he wrote.

He had made more than a beginning. The whole coast was in terror. King Philip sent out contradictory orders that ended in confusion. No shipping dared move, for as Drake's flag captain, Edward Fenner, wrote: "We lie between home and the rest of the king of Spain's ships, so as the body is without the members and they cannot come together."

Then on June 1, 1587, Drake vanished into the blue. This plunged the Spaniards into even greater dismay; no one knew where he had gone or what he meant to do next.

On the morning of June 18, a great carrack, the *San*

Felipe, King Philip's own ship, was swinging near the Azores. She had spent the winter at the Portuguese colony of Mozambique in East Africa, and was making for home under a fair wind. All at once a ship appeared over the horizon and bore down on her. In the waters of the king of Spain, there could be nothing but friends, and the carrack dipped her colors.

Unfortunately for her, it was Drake. No wonder the

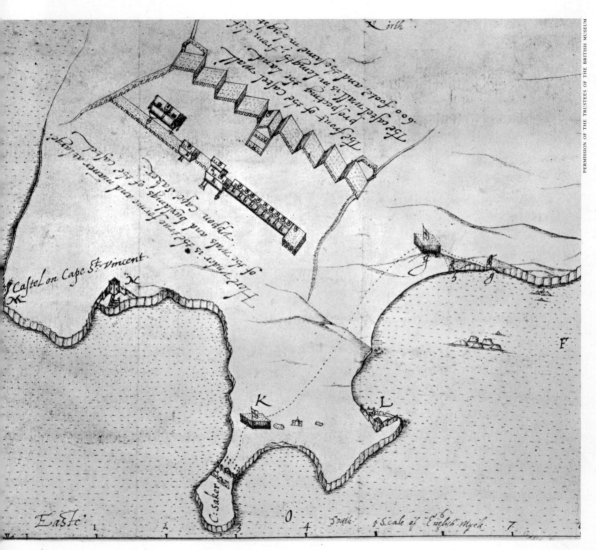

This map of the Cape St. Vincent area in May, 1587, officially ascribed to an "unknown hand," is almost certainly by William Borough, Drake's second in command, who protested his captain's seizure of the cape. With the same attention to detail as the chart on page 79, it gives Drake's route to Sagres ("Saker") and, inverted above, a closer look at the castle's defenses.

Headquarters for the Armada's admiral, the Marquis of Santa Cruz (right), was the great seaport of Lisbon, Portugal's capital. Even in 1582, the year of the engraving below, the broad Tagus River was thronged with sailing vessels and rowboats, and new galleons were already being constructed in the yards (left) that lined its banks.

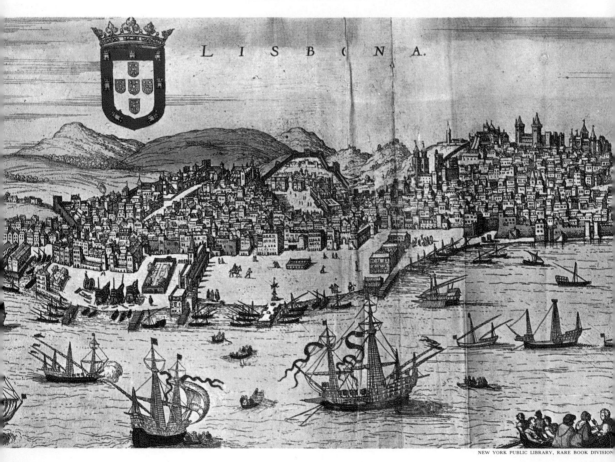

Spaniards believed he had a magic mirror that showed him the movements of all his enemies.

An eyewitness in the *Elizabeth Bonaventure* described the meeting. "We, knowing what she was, would put out no flag until we were within shot of her, [when] we hanged out flags, streamers, and pendants that she might be out of doubt what we were. Which done, we hailed her with cannon shot; and having shot her through divers times, she shot at us." It was an unequal struggle. Drake's guns were too much for the carrack. He sent his flyboat and a pinnace to cut the big ship off. She could do them no harm, for they came in close, and the carrack's guns could not be pointed down so steeply. As the rest of Drake's squadron closed in the merchantman surrendered.

The *San Felipe* was one of the richest prizes ever taken. She was crammed with silk, spices, chests of china and porcelain, bales of velvet, and strongboxes full of jewels and gold. Her ultimate value altogether fell just short of £114,000—a million-dollar haul. It was a splendid climax to three months of work.

This brass instrument with seven dials—for recording tides, feast days, and zodiac signs—was made for Drake in 1569. It may have prompted the magic-mirror tales.

Queen Elizabeth had no cause for complaint, for her share of the treasure was £40,000, nearly one third of the total. And Drake had certainly "impeached" the Spanish war effort most effectively. Months later he learned of the most decisive result of his raid: Santa Cruz had spent his summer on a wild-goose chase.

After the capture of the *San Felipe*, King Philip dared not risk the taking of the Spanish treasure fleet by Drake's raiders. When Santa Cruz reached the Azores in August, after a mad rush to outfit his ships, he found that the English had left two months earlier. By the time he had escorted the treasure fleet safely into harbor and returned to Lisbon with his squadron to rest and refit, it was too late for the Armada to sail in 1587, and its voyage was put off until the spring of 1588.

Drake, however, knew that although he had delayed the Armada, he had not stopped it. "I assure your Honor," he wrote to Walsingham, while still at Cape St. Vincent, "the like preparation was never heard of or known, as the king of Spain hath and daily maketh to invade England. . . . This service which by God's sufferance we have done will breed some alteration of their pretenses; nevertheless, all possible preparations for defense are very expedient to be made." And in a postscript he added the warning, "Prepare in England strongly, and most by sea. Stop him now and stop him ever!"

V   THE ENTERPRISE

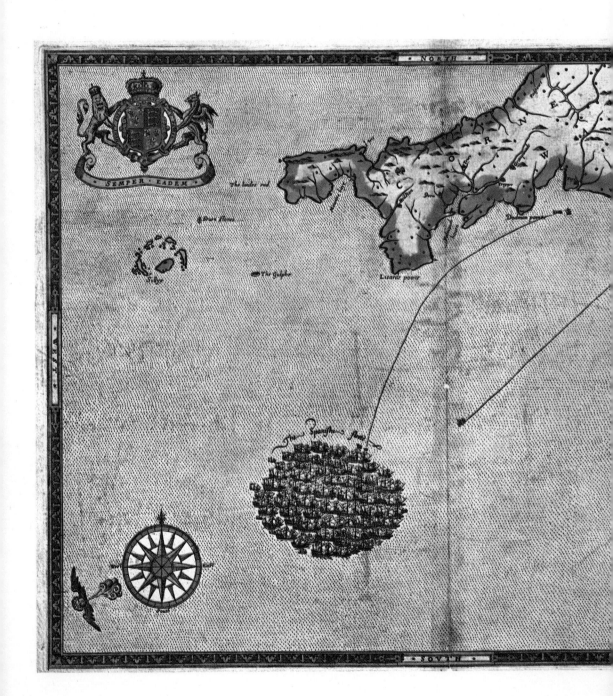

IS LAUNCHED

Drake's success in his raid on the Spanish coast in the summer of 1587 had saved England for that year at least. But this was not immediately obvious to the queen and some of her advisers, who were more complaining than grateful. Lord Burghley insisted that Drake had raided Cadiz against the queen's wishes, saying that "Her Majesty is as yet greatly offended with him."

It may be that Elizabeth really believed she was. Perhaps she hoped that King Philip had had a sharp enough lesson to make him change his plans and that the Armada would not sail. Certainly she was still negotiating peace proposals with the Duke of Parma. Whatever her motives, she ignored Drake's warnings and ordered him to pay off his crews. He was to return the royal ships to the dockyard and their guns to the Tower of London.

But Drake had been right. Although his raid had delayed the Armada, it had not stopped it, and the form it would take was gradually becoming clear. By fall fresh reinforcements had brought Parma's strength up to 30,000 men, and the Dutch reported the assembling of flotillas of flat-bottomed boats and the digging of countless new canals to link his inland forces with the Channel ports. In December, news reached England that Philip, disregarding Santa Cruz' pleas for more time to assemble sailors, ships, and provisions, had told him to get to sea as quickly as he could.

Elizabeth instantly ordered full mobilization of her navy. Then a fresh report came through that the Armada would not sail until spring, and she had the crews reduced by half. A small patrol was sent to join the Dutch in keeping watch off the Netherlands coast, but the rest of her ships sat in harbor while their captains chafed on shore.

Like a swarm of bees, the 124 ships of Philip's Armada gather off the Lizard, at the southern tip of Cornwall, on July 29, 1588. To the right, an English scout from Plymouth turns with the warning "The Spaniards have come!"

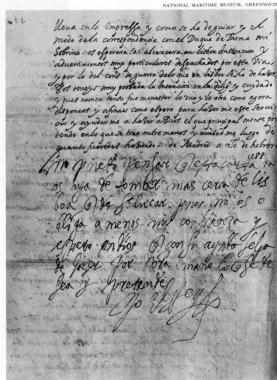

There was good cause for the queen's move. Fleets in the sixteenth century lost far more men from disease and even starvation than by enemy action. With no available means of preserving food other than salting it down, provisions began to rot almost as soon as they were loaded. Water, usually impure when it went into casks, was green with slime by the time it was drunk. The total lack of hygiene on board ship meant that the more men were packed in under full mobilization conditions—overcrowded, undernourished, and unwashed—the quicker they fell sick from the deadly diseases of typhus, scurvy, and food poisoning. Keeping half the crews on land where they could eat fresh food, at their own expense, not only saved money; it saved lives that would be valuable later.

Then, early in March, came news that the Spanish admiral, the Marquis of Santa Cruz, was dead from exhaustion and overwork. He had done his best to get the Armada ready for sea, but the gigantic task had overwhelmed him.

The king had already picked Santa Cruz' successor,

Philip was fortunate in having the able and energetic Duke of Parma (right) as general of his Netherlands army. Bereft of an equally competent admiral by Santa Cruz' sudden death, the king appointed the Duke of Medina Sidonia (far left), a landsman, to command his fleet. The letter at left overrules the duke's timid protests with a postscript, in Philip's handwriting, instructing him to hasten to Lisbon and get the Armada to sea.

Don Alonso Perez de Guzman el Bueno, Duke of Medina Sidonia, a quiet, melancholy man whose chief claim to the post of Captain General of the Ocean Sea was his exalted rank—an important qualification in Spain, where honor and rank counted for so much. Not even the most fiercely proud Spanish grandee could resent serving under him.

Medina Sidonia was an intelligent man who knew perfectly well that he was not qualified to lead the Armada to victory. "I know by experience of the little I have been at sea that I am always seasick and always catch cold," he wrote pathetically to the king. ". . . since I have had no experience either of the sea or of war, I cannot feel that I ought to command so important an enterprise."

But Philip would not listen. He sent a letter to the duke telling him that God would make up any shortcomings he happened to have and insisting that he go at once to Lisbon and get the Enterprise afloat.

In Lisbon, Medina Sidonia found chaos. He was a methodical man, and he at once formed a council to help

The Fleete of Castile whereof Diego Flores de Valdes was Generall, consisted of 14 Galleons and 2 Pinnaces, having in it 2485 Soldiers 1719 Mariners, 384 Canons.

The Fleete of Biscay Comanded by Don Ioan Martinez de Recalde which Consisted of 14 Vessells, 2037 Souldiers, 863 Mariners, 200 Canons.

A unique set of seventeenth-century playing cards illustrates the familiar suits with events that occurred in 1588. Above, the squadrons of Castile and Biscay have become the five and six of hearts.

him get matters into shape. Sensibly, he included in the council three of his squadron commanders, outstanding seamen who would make up for his own lack of ability in this area, and in their hands, work went forward swiftly.

Pedro de Valdes was an experienced captain who had fought the English before and had commanded a squadron during the conquest of Portugal. Miguel de Oquendo was known as the Glory of the Fleet. He was brave and hot-headed and had distinguished himself particularly in the battle of Terceira. The third man was Juan Martinez de Recalde, who had been a fleet commander for sixteen years and had served as Santa Cruz' vice-admiral. He was no longer young, but his skill, valor, and experience made him by far the most valuable sailor in the fleet.

Some changes had been made in the original plans. For one thing, galleys no longer played an important part in the arrangements, probably because Drake's expedition had shown how useless they were against heavy ships. Only four of them were finally included in the fleet, along with four of the new galleasses. Medina Sidonia, like Hawkins, felt that big ship-smashing guns were needed far more than the smaller man-killers. He did his best to get culverins, but although Spanish agents searched the arsenals of Europe for ordnance, he still had to sail with nothing like the numbers he wanted. He ordered twice as much gunpowder as Santa Cruz had listed, and he increased the rounds of shot per gun from thirty to fifty.

He could do little about some of his other problems. The Armada had been in preparation so long that the crews were inevitably dying from poor food and filthy living conditions on board. As usual, in both Spain and England, sailors' pay was in arrears—Philip had not been able to get his loan from the pope. Men deserted in droves, and others had to be drafted in their place. The longer the sailing date was delayed the more the provisions already loaded spoiled and had to be replaced. Drake's sinking of the ships carrying barrel staves at Cape St. Vincent now began to be felt, for there were not enough seasoned barrels for water or food. It was almost impossible, too, for Medina Sidonia to find supplies of salt meat, and especially of salt fish—Drake's raid had nearly wiped out the tunny-fishing fleet.

Toward the end of April, however, everything was ready. It was a formidable navy that had been assembled, even though it did not contain the vast numbers of ships and men that Santa Cruz had once hoped for. The first line of battle was under the personal direction of Medina

Sidonia, assisted in his decisions by Diego Flores de Valdes. Flores de Valdes, a cousin of Pedro de Valdes, had been a fleet commander for twenty years and should have made a fine chief of staff for Medina Sidonia. But he was disliked by everyone who knew him—scarcely a qualification for a good leader. His official command was the ten big galleons from the Indian Guard, normally used to escort the treasure ships across the Atlantic. These, with the nine galleons of the royal Portuguese navy, a splendid Italian warship, the *San Francesco*, the four galleasses, and four powerful greatships, made up the first line.

The second line of battle contained forty well-armed merchant ships, some of them extremely large. These were divided into four squadrons, each named for the province of Spain that had provided it. Recalde led the Biscayan squadron from the north of Spain; Oquendo commanded the Guipuzcoans from the Basque country; and Valdes was in charge of the Andalusians from the south. The fourth, the Levant squadron, from Barcelona and Philip's possessions in Italy, was led by Martin de Bertendona, a trustworthy officer. There were also twenty-three storeships and thirty-four pinnaces and other small vessels used as messengers and scouts. Following Spanish custom there were only 10,000 sailors (2,000 of them galley slaves) to work the 130 ships and 19,000 soldiers to do the real fighting; barely 150 gunners handled the inferior work of firing at the enemy.

King Philip had outlined the basic plan a few years earlier. The Armada would sweep up the Channel, crush any English ships that tried to oppose it, and join with Parma. It would then convoy him and his troops in their barges to the southern coast of England. After that, Medina Sidonia would attack any English ships he found at sea or in harbors. The English fleet was reported by the king's spies to be very weak. Nevertheless, in order to keep to the timetable, the Armada was not to look for battle until it had met with Parma.

Perhaps Philip was uncertain of his commander's ability. He may well have been nervous that anything should go wrong with this incredibly complicated operation on which he had lavished so much time and money and for which he had taken so many risks. Whatever his reasons, Philip did not make the unfortunate Medina Sidonia's task any easier by deluging him with precise instructions anticipating almost every eventuality that could possibly befall him—except what in fact did.

On April 25, 1588, the Duke of Medina Sidonia went in

The Fleete of Portugall consisting of 12 Vessels, in wch were 3330 Souldiers, 1233 Marriners, 300 Canons

Don Alphonso Duke of Medina, Cheife Comander of ye Spanish Fleete & John Martin Recalde a great Seaman.

The loyal Englishman who engraved these cards allowed the Portuguese squadron an honorable position as seven of hearts but contemptuously gave Medina Sidonia and Recalde the knave of clubs.

solemn procession to the Cathedral of Lisbon where he received the standard of the Enterprise, which bore the arms of Spain between a Virgin and a Crucifixion, with the motto "Arise, O Lord, and vindicate Thy cause." The Archbishop of Lisbon blessed the Armada and its banner while the soldiers and sailors who filled the huge cathedral and all the streets outside it knelt reverently. Then a joyous salute was fired. (As Philip had carefully instructed, it was a small salute—to save gunpowder.) Two weeks from this great day the order was given for the start of the crusade that would bring England back to Catholicism.

Early in March, Drake, leashed in at Plymouth with the western squadron of ships, heard rumors from his scouts that the Armada would be launched by the end of that month. He at once began begging the queen in letter after letter to be allowed to sail out against it. As ever, he understood the value of striking the first blow. He proposed sailing instantly for Lisbon where, if the Spaniards came out, "they shall be fought with, and I hope, through the goodness of God, in such sort as shall hinder [their] quiet passage into England. . . . The advantage of time and place in all martial actions is half a victory. . . ."

Early in May, Drake was at last called to London to discuss his plan. The queen caught the spark of his enthusiasm. This was her most daring captain, after all, the man who had singed the beard of King Philip, captured Cartagena, and made himself the terror of Spain. She decided upon action.

On May 10 her council sent a letter to the Lord Admiral, who was patrolling the Netherlands coast with the Channel guard, instructing him to provision all available ships and get them to sea. His orders left no doubt that England was to take the offensive. It was high time. The day before Lord Howard received his letter, Medina Sidonia had given the Armada the command to sail.

The Enterprise, however, was having trouble. For almost three weeks bad weather had prevented it from getting beyond the mouth of Lisbon harbor. When the ships were finally able to set forth, they had to go at a snail's pace to let the storeships keep up. It took the Armada another three weeks to creep as far as Corunna, at the northwest tip of Spain. Here Medina Sidonia ordered his ships to put in for fresh water and provisions, which were already in desperately short supply.

Not quite half the Armada was able to anchor before night fell. The rest remained in open water, waiting for

In this engraving of Lisbon harbor, about the time the Armada set forth, great galleons take crews aboard, and barrels of supplies line the bustling wharves.

morning. But in the middle of the night a terrible storm arose. When it died away a day and a half later, it had blown seventy Spanish ships far into the Atlantic.

Medina Sidonia sent out his scouting pinnaces to round up the missing ships. Four days later, with twenty-eight big ships and two of the galleasses still unaccounted for, the duke held a council of war. All but one of his commanders voted to stay in Corunna and wait for them to return.

Because in 1588 England had not yet adopted the revised Gregorian calendar, this playing card has the Armada setting sail on May 20 instead of the now-accepted May 30.

The strong winds that in May had kept the Armada from getting away from Lisbon had carried Lord Howard down to Plymouth with forty ships.

Drake had been waiting impatiently for him, and some Englishmen predicted trouble when the two met. It had been at Drake's insistence that the fleet had been forced into readiness, and when Philip of Spain wrote dispatches to Medina Sidonia, he spoke as though Drake were commander in chief of the English fleet. Men who knew his impatience with authority thought he might well refuse to serve under Howard.

They need not have worried. For Drake the important thing was that there should be a fleet ready to fight the Spaniards. It would have been exceedingly unlikely in that age for a commoner to be put in command of it. Queen Elizabeth, like King Philip, chose noblemen to fill the highest offices of state. Lord Howard's father had been Lord Admiral before him. He himself had only once been in combat, but he knew how to take advice, and he knew when he needed it. He was intensely proud of his ships and their crews. Best of all, he had the ability to make men work together smoothly and efficiently. He brought with him, for Drake, the queen's commission as vice-admiral of the fleet. It was all Drake had wished for—next to the chance to fight his old enemy, the king of Spain.

With the thirty ships he had waiting at Plymouth, he sailed out to greet Howard. Both flotillas saluted each other. As the guns roared out and the men lining the bulwarks cheered, Howard ceremoniously struck the vice-admiral's flag, which was flying next to his own on the *Ark Royal*, and sent it over to Drake's ship, the *Revenge*.

Drake was now all for pushing out to catch the Spaniards, but the fleet was too short of food to make the voyage. While Lord Howard was writing urgent letters to London imploring that the victualing ships be sent, fishermen brought him word that the Armada had left Lisbon with "hundreds of ships." Drake and Howard put to sea but were driven back by a fierce west wind. For three weeks they fretted in Plymouth harbor, praying alternately for the wind to change and for their supplies to arrive.

On July 2 the victualing ships arrived, and the wind veered to the northeast, just right for sailing south to Spain. Intelligence reports made it clear that the wind that had kept the English in harbor had also dispersed the Spaniards outside Corunna. Howard decided to make for the Spanish coast and seek them out. He and Drake set forth and had nearly sighted Cape Finisterre when a full gale sprang up from the southwest, and they had to turn back. The same wind that blew them home could speed the Spaniards on their way, and there was more than a chance they could slip by if the defenders were too far from the entry to the Channel. Howard was just in time. As his anchors rattled into Plymouth harbor, on July 22, Medina Sidonia was signaling his reunited fleet to head for England.

On Friday, July 29, according to a commonly accepted story, Drake, Howard, and some of the other officers were playing bowls on Plymouth Hoe, a long strip of grass overlooking the sound. A Captain Fleming, commander of a scouting vessel, came running up to report that the Armada had been sighted off the Lizard, the southernmost tip of the Cornish coast. With the wind behind them the Spaniards could sail swiftly up to Plymouth, a matter of fifty miles or so, and trap the English fleet where it lay at anchor. Drake's reply is so typical of him that the story may indeed be true: "We have time enough to finish the game and beat the Spaniards too."

Drake knew the tides in the sound as well as any man. It is probable that the tide was running into the harbor, which, added to that strong southwest breeze, would have made it extremely difficult to sail out right away. Time was needed too in order to load supplies and get the crews

Seymour Lucas' famous picture of the English captains interrupted in their game of bowls on Plymouth Hoe by news of the Armada's approach was painted after careful research on Elizabethan portraits. His model for Lord Howard, who stands with Drake (bowl in hand), was obviously the overleaf portrait.

aboard. But by evening the tide had turned, and Howard led out fifty-four ships; the rest were still taking on supplies.

Now the English showed their seamanship. John Hawkins, who was serving Howard as rear admiral of the fleet, must have looked on with the pride of a father as his new design—with low rakish bow and cut-down sterncastle—proved its worth. One by one, in the dusk, the English ships warped out into open water and then began beating out to sea against the wind. As they passed the Eddystone Rocks they could see, far off, the flicker of topsails against the western sky, where the enemy lay hove to off the Lizard. Medina Sidonia was holding a war council. At sea the wind dropped; Howard ordered mainsails lowered, and his fleet waited under bare poles. He had turned the tables on the Spaniards. Instead of being trapped in Plymouth, the English were now to the south of the Spanish fleet, ready to take advantage of the wind as soon as it sprang up again.

Medina Sidonia had had a rough passage from Corunna. His four galleys could not face the huge seas and had been forced to run for shelter to the French coast. Although one of his powerful armed merchant ships had disappeared during a gale, the rest of the Enterprise was intact. He had held his council of war because he felt sure Drake must be in Plymouth harbor. Lord Howard he believed to be still patrolling the Dutch coast. The duke's orders were clear: he was not to look for a fight but was to sail on to join Parma or find a place where he could wait until he had made arrangements for their rendezvous. Some of his captains wanted to try to catch Drake in Plymouth, but they were overruled. Medina Sidonia sent his scouts out ahead and moved his fleet eastward. As they came within sight of land, watchers on hill after hill set light to the huge bonfires that had been lying ready-piled for weeks. Along the coast and far inland the warning beacons flared. Within hours the queen and most of her subjects the length and breadth of the country knew that the Spaniards had come at last.

On Saturday, July 30, the Armada anchored off Dodman Point, halfway between the Lizard and the city of Plymouth. Lookouts could see the white gleam of sails far off to leeward—that is, in the direction toward which the wind was blowing. The duke's scouts brought back an English fishing boat, and Medina Sidonia now learned that Howard

England's Lord Admiral, Lord Howard of Effingham (opposite), was painted with his fleet in 1619. Above, beacons dot the Cornish coast in 1588.

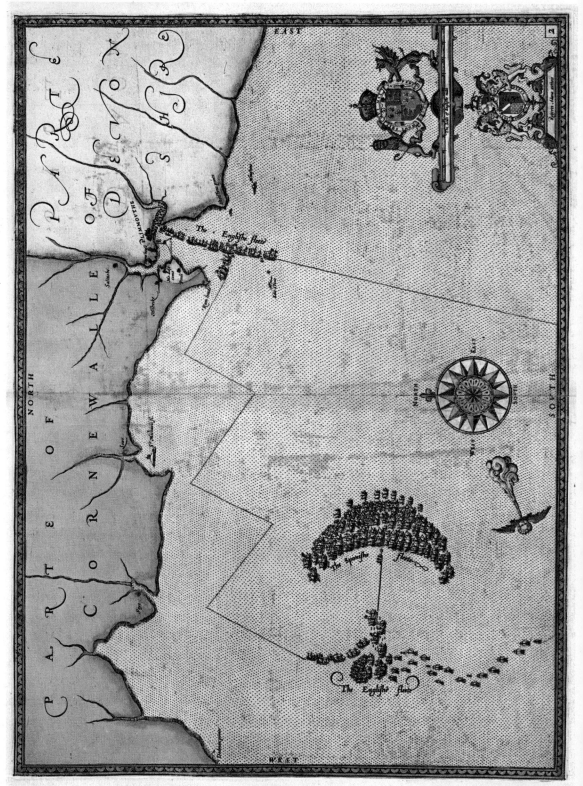

100

and Drake were together and that their joint fleet had come out of Plymouth. They were somewhere at sea, and he thought it was their sails he had seen. That night, he readied his ships for an attack the next morning. But he had no fear of it, for the wind was at his back, and he was sure he could bear down upon the English and trap them against their own coast.

But as the sky brightened, the Duke of Medina Sidonia saw a long line of ships coming from behind him, their sails filled with the same southwest wind that was to have given him the advantage. The ships he had seen the night before were the eleven that had to remain in Plymouth to finish victualing. Exchanging shots at extreme range with the foremost Spaniards, the eleven latecomers now raced around the vanguard of the Armada to rejoin the rest of the English fleet. The sun rose, and now for the first time each side could plainly see the strength of its opponent.

Before the English lay an enormous number of ships, more sail than anyone there had ever seen gathered together at one time. Even with the losses from weather, there remained well over 120, although as both Drake and Howard noted in their dispatches, only about half were true warships. At a signal from the flagship, this whole vast fleet swept into battle formation, turning completely around so they could take an attack from the south instead of the north, where they had expected the English ships to be. It was a remarkable feat of discipline.

The Spanish formation was shaped roughly like a great crescent. In the center were the twenty galleons of Castile and Portugal, the main battle, as it was called, with Medina Sidonia's flagship, the *San Martin*, at their head. Two of the galleasses were probably here as well, while the other two reinforced the wings. The storeships were behind the main battle but also in the center. And stretching in an arc to guard the rear of this mass of vessels were four squadrons, each with about ten greatships and armed merchantmen. On the left wing were Recalde's Biscayans, then the Andalusians under Pedro de Valdes; on the right were the Guipuzcoans under Oquendo and the Levanters led by Martin de Bertendona. Tough old Recalde, in the *San Juan*, had

Pedro de Valdes (above) commanded the Andalusian squadron; Juan Martinez de Recalde (below) was in charge of the entire left wing.

The chart opposite shows the main English fleet sailing south and west from Plymouth to get windward of the Spaniards as latecomers tack alongshore (at left) to join it. At center the tiny Disdain *fires the challenge.* OVERLEAF: *In a period painting, the two fleets hammer away at each other.*

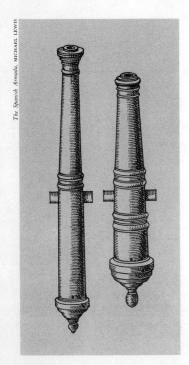

Guns played an all-important part in the Armada campaign. The culverin (at left) was the long-range weapon favored by the English; the Spaniards' preference for the heavy cannon (right), effective only at close range, led to their defeat.

command of the whole left wing, while the right was commanded by a young nobleman, Don Alonso de Leyva.

The Spaniards saw a far larger and stronger fleet than they had expected. Although a final tally listed 197 ships, great and small, serving with Howard, only some sixty warships were with him now. In terms of fighting vessels, however, the two sides were about equal. Compared to Spanish ships, the English looked small, but in terms of weight, which is how a warship must be judged, the English were quite as strong as the Spaniards, and Martin Frobisher's 1,100-ton *Triumph* was larger than anything in the Armada. All told, Howard had five ships of 800 tons or more to Medina Sidonia's eight, but in ships of medium weight or less, the English were if anything superior. What was much more to the point, they were handier sailers and could use the wind better. And, as was soon to be shown, one of their strongest advantages lay in their guns and the men who worked them. The English fleet carried some 14,000 men as sailors and 1,500 as soldiers (compared with the Spaniards' 8,000 mariners and 19,000 soldiers). There was no separate category for gunners, since to the English sailor, firing a gun was part of his work as a mariner. On the English ships everyone worked as a team in a common cause: the defense of his country, his home, and his family against invasion.

The English fleet advanced in a long line. Like the chivalrous nobleman he was, Howard delivered his challenge: a tiny pinnace, the *Disdain*, shot out ahead of the fleet and fired off one of her little popguns. It was the signal for the battle. The day was Sunday, July 31, 1588.

The English swept across the right wing of the crescent. Some of them, led by the Lord Admiral in the *Ark Royal*, exchanged broadsides with Bertendona's squadron, and although the Spaniards kept trying to close in, they were held off by the English culverins with their longer range. Meanwhile, another group of English sailed over to the left wing of the crescent. Drake, in the *Revenge*, was at their head, and with him were Frobisher in the huge *Triumph* and John Hawkins in the *Victory*. Once again the longer range of the English guns told. On this wing, Recalde tried to close with at least one of his foes so he could bring his heavy cannons into play. But the English kept out of range and hammered away until his *San Juan* sailed back into formation.

The English broke off the action about noon. Medina Sidonia at once tried to take the offensive, to get to windward of the enemy and attack. But the English had no difficulty outmaneuvering him. "They still keep the weather gauge [the position to windward]," noted the Spanish log, "and their ships are so fast and nimble they can do anything they like with them."

In fact, the wind was to be the decisive element in the long-drawn-out battle. Sailing ships could operate at their best when the wind was strongly behind them, filling their sails and giving them speed to bear down on their foes. Once they fell to leeward of the enemy, the only remedy was to turn into the wind and tack from side to side, getting its benefit at an angle to move them forward—much slower, of course, than when running before the wind. The Spanish ships had lost the advantage of the windward position, and unless the wind changed, they would never again be able to mount an effective attack.

The afternoon lull was broken by a gigantic explosion. The greatship *San Salvador*, in Oquendo's squadron, blew up. The story got about later that a gunner on the ship who had been unjustly punished had tossed a lighted torch into the powder magazine and then jumped overboard. However it happened, the *San Salvador* was ablaze and severely damaged. Medina Sidonia at once turned back to transfer the wounded and arrange for her to be taken in tow.

As the ship burned, Howard launched another attack. He was met by Recalde and his ships, followed by Pedro de Valdes. Somehow, in the movement, Valdes' ship, *Nuestra Señora del Rosario*, rammed another vessel. The *Rosario*'s bowsprit was broken off, and her foremast stay snapped. Drifting helplessly, she began falling behind.

Medina Sidonia, busy arranging the rescue of the *San Salvador*, saw the *Rosario*'s plight. He sailed the *San Martin* alongside and put a cable over so he could tow away the stricken ship. The seas were growing rougher, and the cable broke. Pedro de Valdes refused to leave his ship. Diego Flores de Valdes, no friend to his cousin, argued with Medina Sidonia that he must abandon the *Rosario* or risk all the rest of his fleet in the gathering dusk. Reluctantly, Medina Sidonia at last left the *Rosario* to her fate.

If the first round seemed to have gone to the English, they had certainly not won the quick victory they hoped for. The Armada, still in unbroken formation and almost unharmed, went on its way eastward up the Channel, potentially as dangerous as ever. Drake sent word to Lord Henry Seymour that "there hath passed some cannon shot between some of our fleet and some of them, and as far as we perceive they are determined to sell their lives with blows." The real fighting was still to come.

An explosion aboard the greatship San Salvador *caused such damage that the Spaniards were forced to abandon the ship to the English.*

VI   "GOD BREATHED..."

On that Sunday evening, July 31, the English captains met in council on the Lord Admiral's flagship. It seemed probable to them that the Duke of Medina Sidonia would try to find a sheltered spot somewhere along the English coast where he could anchor until he heard from Parma that all was ready for their meeting. One good possibility might be the northern shore of the Isle of Wight. There was a chance too that the Spaniards, if they could find a protected anchorage and if they were left alone, might land soldiers on English soil, burn and pillage, and help themselves to any available supplies. Such a move would hearten the Span-

In Hendrik Cornelisz Vroom's spirited painting of the battle off the Isle of Wight, the San Martin *(left), flying Medina Sidonia's red Armada standard, engages the* Ark Royal *(right). Vroom included two galleys (at far right), although none in fact was present.*

iards immensely, while giving a serious blow to England.

To the English seamen the best plan appeared to be to follow the Armada, pressing hard on its heels with the southwest wind, and to give it no chance of resting or finding such a snug harbor. Drake was chosen to lead the English fleet in pursuit, and the other vessels prepared to sail on through the night, guiding themselves by the light of the *Revenge*'s big stern lantern.

For a while all went well. Then suddenly the lookout on the flagship, which was following immediately behind the *Revenge*, lost sight of the flickering light. All was dark for a time, and then the light appeared again, farther away. Howard hastened to catch up. But at dawn on Monday, August 1, the Lord Admiral discovered that he was fol-

lowing not Drake's lantern but that of a Spanish ship and that he was almost within the crescent of the Armada. The rest of his fleet was far behind, and he swiftly turned back to it. Drake had vanished and did not appear again until much later in the day.

His excuse was not strange to those who knew him. During the night, he said, he had seen sails in the distance. Thinking they were Spaniards trying to slip by him, he had put out his lantern so that the ships behind him would not follow and had then given chase. The sails turned out to be those of some German ships, and he had let them go. However, by the curious good fortune that always seemed to guide him to worthwhile prizes, he had "just happened" to come across the *Rosario*, still wallowing in the waves. Her captain, Pedro de Valdes, had repaired neither her bowsprit nor her foremast. And when he found who his challenger was, he made no effort to engage the *Revenge* in battle. Instead, he surrendered to Drake, who thus found himself in possession of a fine, fully armed ship worth a great deal of money, 55,000 ducats of it in the captain's sea chest.

Drake's action was typical of these sea captains, to whom war was not only a patriotic duty but a means of making money. Frobisher's snarling reaction, "He thinks to cheat us of our shares!" was partly the result of his longstanding enmity with Drake and partly the envy of an ex-privateer who saw another man profiting instead of himself. No one seems to have condemned Drake for abandoning his duties as guide to the fleet to seek out a prize. The Lord Admiral did not reprimand him; indeed, to many of the captains, the capture of an enemy squadron commander and his flagship was most cheerful news. (Strangely enough, Valdes was never reprimanded either, when he finally returned to Spain from captivity, for surrendering his ship without a fight. In another age he would have been court-martialed; so, probably, would Drake.)

A little later the English took another prize, the *San Salvador*. Although her fires had burned out, she was beyond repair and had been cut adrift. Curiously, there was still a great store of usable powder and shot aboard, which Howard thankfully took for his vessels.

That night, both fleets anchored almost within gunshot of each other, not far from a promontory called Portland Bill. Early in the morning of Tuesday, August 2, the wind shifted to the east. This almost brought disaster to the English, since the Spaniards now had them to leeward. Howard at first turned his ships toward shore, hoping to

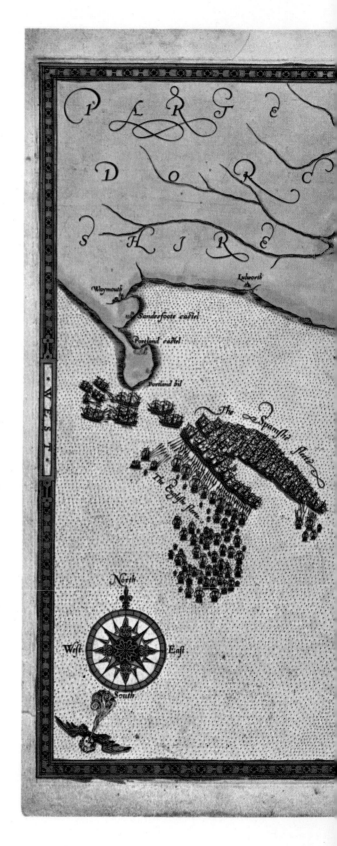

Martin Frobisher (above) and his ships were cut off while trying to edge past the Armada at Portland Bill, far left on the chart at right. In the next day's action (right of center) Frobisher led one of the English squadrons in pursuit.

111

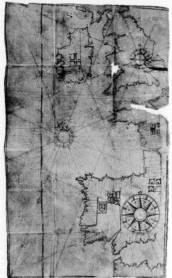

This battered map of Europe's Atlantic coast, much thumbed around the entrance to the Channel, comes from Drake's own pocket book. Its sketchiness makes plain how much lore a skilled mariner like Sir Francis had to carry in his head.

slip past the enemy's left wing. When the Spaniards headed them off, the English began tacking out to sea to get around their right wing. At once, Bertendona's squadron, on the extreme right, intercepted, and a lively battle began, with quantities of ammunition fired on both sides.

Martin Frobisher and five other English ships had not turned back to sea with the others but had continued to edge around the Spanish left wing near the shore. Now they were dangerously close to the jutting sands of Portland Bill. The four galleasses, under the command of Hugo de Moncada, a captain every bit as headstrong and fiery as Frobisher himself, cornered them there. A hot fight developed, the Spaniards as usual trying to get near enough to board; but the English long guns kept them away, their shot smashing through the light bulwarks and killing many men at the oars. Still, Frobisher was in great danger, for the galleasses could maneuver with both oars and sails and were strong enough to give him a pounding.

Then, suddenly, the wind swung back into the southwest. Through the clouds of gunsmoke a mass of ships, their guns roaring, swooped down on the main body of Spaniards and forced them to draw off. Drake and his squadron had made their way out to sea, expecting the wind to change; now they came back with it behind them. The right wing of the Armada recoiled, and at Medina Sidonia's signal, the galleasses on the left stopped baiting Frobisher and joined the rest of the fleet in fighting off the new threat.

The duke was leading sixteen of his first-line galleons to meet the English admiral when he saw that Recalde— bravely in advance of his squadron as usual—had been cut off and was under heavy fire. Medina Sidonia had lost one squadron commander in Pedro de Valdes; he could not afford to lose Recalde, the best of them all. At his orders, all the other galleons turned back to rescue Recalde, and the *San Martin* prepared to meet Howard alone. The Spaniards expected that a proper naval action would now be fought. The two flagships would lie side by side, exchanging broadsides; then they would grapple, and the soldiers would decide the issue by a hand-to-hand combat. The *San Martin* backed her sails and fired a shot to challenge the *Ark Royal*.

But the English had invented a new way of fighting at sea, a way that had doomed the old method. Instead of coming to close quarters, Howard swung his ship and let go a whole broadside at the *San Martin*. Then he sailed on. Behind him came the rest of his ships, one after the other in what was later to be called line ahead, each firing in turn. For almost an hour the *San Martin* received their fire and returned it most courageously. But the English were still shooting at too long a range to do much damage. Their culverins were too light to break up the four-foot timbers of the *San Martin* unless they came to point-blank range and risked the fire of her much heavier cannons. Meanwhile, "at least 500 cannon balls," as the duke later reported, hulled the ship in several places, carried away some of her rigging and her flagstaff, and killed fifty men aboard her.

At last, Oquendo came up with his squadron, and as more and more galleons hurried to cluster around their flagship, Howard gave the signal to retire.

Thus the third day of the battle ended without a decisive action. The Armada still held together, not seriously hurt. Both sides had developed a good deal of respect for each other. The Spaniards marveled at the speed of the English gunnery and at the amazing swiftness of their ships. The English saw that it was not going to be easy to stop this mighty and courageous foe.

The greatest problem at the moment was ammunition. In spite of all Drake's warnings and Howard's pleas, the English ships had not received as much powder and shot as they had asked for, and the rapid firing that so impressed the Spaniards had used up much of the supply. On Wednesday, August 3, Howard sent his small boats ashore to collect all the roundshot and powder they could scrape up.

While he was waiting for these desperately needed supplies, the Lord Admiral reorganized his fleet. From each port along Howard's route, volunteers eager to do their part in England's defense had been bringing small private ships to join him, so that he now had over a hundred sail. Most of them had little experience of battle, and their very enthusiasm made them unruly and hard to control. For that matter, so were his regular captains, who had grown accustomed to acting independently and making their own decisions. Much of the waste of ammunition was due to the lack of regulated firing.

Taking a lesson from the excellent discipline and organization of the Spanish fleet, Howard broke his force into four squadrons. One was to be under his command, the second under Drake, the third under that cool old veteran Hawkins, and the fourth would be captained by the courageous but brash Frobisher.

That day was relatively quiet, if only because neither side had much ammunition to spare. There was one short, sharp engagement when the *Gran Grifon*, the galleon that

In his dashing, hard-to-read hand, Drake writes from aboard the Revenge *to the queen's secretary. In the eighth line he hopes to God that "the prince of parma and the Duke of Sidonya shall not shake hands this fewe dayes," and a postscript asks for "munycyon and vittuall."*

led the Spanish storeships, lagged behind the rest and was caught by the watchful Drake. Before Recalde's squadron could rescue her from his guns, she suffered many casualties: seventy killed and as many wounded.

Thursday, August 4, found both sides becalmed off the southeast tip of the Isle of Wight, an important and, in fact, crucial spot for the Armada. The English had been right in their guess: the Spaniards needed a safe anchorage in which to wait for news from the Netherlands. Despite a stream of messengers telling Parma to prepare, asking him for fresh ammunition, and requesting information about his plans, Medina Sidonia had had no word from his fellow commander in chief.

The big Isle of Wight shelters the Solent, a five-mile-wide channel between the island and the mainland, and

Behind a screen of fighting ships England prepared for an invasion. Even east-coast towns like Great Yarmouth rebuilt out-of-date fortifications (below, left), and although life went on much as usual, armed galleons guarded the bay.

the Spanish captains, at their council of war off the Lizard, had decided to wait there until they knew that Parma was ready. If they could land on the island, they might be able to hold the calm waters of the Solent for their own. The English, for their part, were determined not to let the Spaniards seize a foothold on their soil.

Hawkins opened the action that morning. A great Portuguese galleon and a storeship were lying a little away from the rest of the Armada, and Hawkins made up his mind to try for one of them. Since there was no wind to speak of, he had his boats tow the *Victory* into range. As soon as he opened fire, three of the galleasses came rowing out to oppose him, along with the *Rata Coronada*, the great carrack belonging to the right-wing commander, Don Alonso de Leyva. The galleasses were at their best in this

weather, and soon musket fire was spattering around Hawkins' boats and wounding men on board the *Victory* herself. Lord Howard got his own boats busy and had the *Ark Royal* towed over to join the fighting. "There were many good shots made," he wrote later in his report. Eventually, however, the galleasses were able to get themselves and the two laggards back into the shelter of the fleet formation.

Over on the English left wing there was an almost exact repetition of what had happened at Portland Bill. Martin Frobisher had pushed too far ahead and had been cut off near the shore of the Isle of Wight. Eleven ships' boat crews were straining at their oars, trying to tow him, but the 1,100-ton *Triumph* was a fearful weight to move. In this predicament he was seen by Medina Sidonia's flagship, and as the *San Martin* drew closer, the wind sprang up from the southeast, blowing Frobisher farther inshore. Other Spaniards hoisted all sail and closed in, certain that the huge *Triumph* must be the English flagship and that they would catch the Lord Admiral himself. Then the wind came to the rescue again: it blew strongly and steadily from the southwest. The *Triumph*'s sails flapped and filled. "She began to slip away from us," said the Spanish log. "She got out so swiftly that the galleon *San Juan* and another quick sailer—the speediest vessel in the Armada—although they chased her, appeared to be standing still."

As the wind swung round and strengthened, it brought with it an English squadron that bore straight for the closest Spanish ships, those on the right wing. Drake and Hawkins, who knew every bit of that coast and its weather, were repeating Drake's Portland Bill maneuver. They had gone out to sea and circled around, waiting for the wind to veer. Now, with the wind filling their sails, they roared down upon the right point of the Spanish crescent, which gave way before them. Worse still, the Spaniards, as they retreated, found themselves being pushed slowly north toward the dangerous reefs and shoals of the Ower Banks. But Medina Sidonia had seen what was happening. Firing his guns to attract attention, he set out to head off his ships and lead them to safety in deeper water. "We who were there," says the account of a Spanish captain, "were driven into a corner so that if the duke had not gone about with his flagship . . . we should have been vanquished that day."

The English were jubilant. Although the Armada still sailed on in its fortresslike formation, the Spaniards could no longer make a landing on the Isle of Wight. Indeed, they were already well on their way toward the narrow part of

The Spaniards dispatching Messingers to the Prince of Parma requiring him forthwith to joyn himselfe with them.

The L.d Admirall Howard Knighting Thomas Howard, the Lord Sheffild, Rog.t Townsend Iohn Hawkins, and Martin Forbisher for their good service

The Armada playing cards catalogue some events in the week-long voyage up the Channel. On August 5, as Medina Sidonia dispatched messengers begging Parma to join him (top), Lord Howard knighted six English commanders on the deck of the Ark Royal (bottom).

the Channel, where there was no good anchorage to hold them. With no word yet from Parma, they were forced to keep moving. On the deck of the *Ark Royal* next morning (Friday, August 5), Howard used his privilege as Lord Admiral to knight Hawkins, Frobisher, and four other officers for their part in the action.

That same day some trickles of powder and shot came to Howard from the mainland, including broken-up plowshares and other bits of iron that could be used as grapeshot to sweep the enemy decks. Local authorities sent whatever they could spare—the fact was that even England's main store of powder and shot in the Tower of London was running low after four days of constant fighting. Instead of ammunition, the queen sent a number of musketeers, and these Howard sent back. He had no intention of getting close enough for musket combat with the Spaniards, and he needed no extra mouths to feed from the few days' food supply left to his fleet.

One consolation was that no one was supplying Medina Sidonia with anything at all. The steady pursuit was beginning to tell on the Spaniards. Their spirits were low; their ammunition, food, and water lower still. Medina Sidonia tried to speak cheerfully of each engagement, but the facts were that the Armada had lost seven good ships through bad luck and bad weather and had suffered more than the English from the exchanges of cannon fire. They were now nearing the trickiest part of the Channel, the weather was growing threatening with rain and mounting waves, and behind them the English still stubbornly came on. Medina Sidonia had to find a harbor, and he had to learn what Parma's plans were.

Late in the afternoon of Saturday, August 6, the Armada dropped anchor outside Calais, on the coast of France. As if it had been rehearsed, the English at once did the same, a long culverin shot—less than two miles—away. Medina Sidonia hastily sent off fresh letters to Parma, imploring him to send whatever supplies of shot he could spare and demanding to know when he would be ready to come out.

That evening, Lord Henry Seymour, with five royal galleons and thirty other ships, came sailing up to reinforce the English fleet. They had been keeping watch for Parma off the Dutch coast, and though they were short of food they carried plenty of ammunition, which was welcome news to Lord Howard. He now had 140 ships and superiority of numbers over the Spaniards. Replacing Seymour's patrol to the north were thirty small but tough Dutch vessels, the Sea

The Spaniards lying at Anchor nere Cales and ye English Admirall ridzing within a Shott of Great Ordnance, the English Navy consisting at this time of 140. Ships.

The Ld. Hen: Seymor wth 40 English and Dutch Ships keeping the Coast of the Netherlands to hinder ye Prince of Parma's coming forth.

On August 6 the Spanish and English fleets both anchored outside Calais (top), each wondering if the French garrison would remain neutral or not. That night, Lord Seymour's Channel patrol (bottom) reinforced Howard, giving him the strength for a major attack.

117

Beggars' fleet under their capable commander Justin of Nassau. Parma could not move against England while they kept their station.

On Sunday, August 7, Lord Howard held another council in the great cabin of the *Ark Royal*. Despite the English strength, the situation was disturbing. All day there had been a coming and going of messenger boats between the Armada and the shore. Was it possible that the French Catholic city of Calais might aid the Spaniards in their crusade? What word had Medina Sidonia received from the Duke of Parma? All might be lost if the Armada could find the resting place so far denied it, and provisions and ammunition too. The problem was to get the Spaniards out of Calais harbor and keep them moving. There seemed only one way to pry the Armada loose: that was to use fireships.

Fire was the chief terror of commanders of wooden ves-

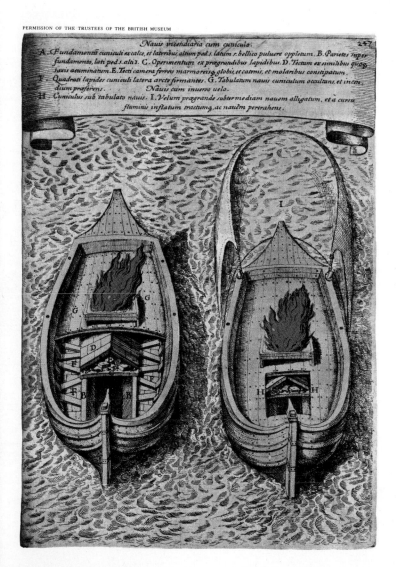

The English decision to use fireships against the Spaniards anchored outside Calais was the crucial moment of the Armada campaign. The 1640 engraving at left shows the classic method of preparing them: holds are caulked against leaks with chalk and then filled with powder, millstones, and iron chains, to explode with deadly effect when set afire. On the boat at right is a submerged sail that will fill with the tide and draw the floating bomb along. Lacking time for such refinements, the English simply set small warships on fire, directed them at the enemy, then jumped clear into waiting ships' boats.

sels. Fireships—boats without crews, filled with oil and pitch, then set on fire and allowed to drift on wind and tide into the midst of an enemy fleet—had been used by the Spaniards against Hawkins at San Juan de Ulua and against Drake at Cadiz. Particularly deadly ones, crammed with explosives and with clockwork fuses that made them into primitive bombs, had been used by the Dutch against the Spaniards during the defense of Antwerp three years earlier. One of them had killed eight hundred men and had devastated a mile-square area, and every Spaniard in the fleet knew the story of the "devil ships" of Antwerp. There was no time now for the English to prepare anything so complicated; ordinary fireships would have to serve.

Drake contributed a ship of his own, the 200-ton *Thomas*. Hawkins followed suit with one of his ships. Six more were found, and two experienced captains were chosen to oversee the hazardous work of loading the vessels and starting them off. Their guns were double-loaded so that when they grew red hot they would explode and add to the confusion. The ships were stuffed with faggots soaked in tar, and after some hours of hard labor all was ready.

Aboard the other fleet there had been a dismal suspicion that something unpleasant was afoot—"a great presentiment of evil from that devilish people and their arts," wrote one Spaniard gloomily. The messenger boats from shore had brought nothing but bad news. Parma was far inland at Bruges, nowhere near the port of Dunkirk, where he should have been. Although he still promised that everything would be ready at the first good opportunity, Medina Sidonia's special messenger reported that so far nothing had been done, no men had been embarked, no barges were gathering, and in his opinion Parma would not be ready for another two weeks at least.

The Duke of Parma, who had originally proposed an invasion of England, had been telling the king for a year that he must have a deepwater port for his rendezvous with Medina Sidonia. He had no warships to escort his men out to join the Armada, and without protection they would be helpless targets for the waiting English and the Dutch. Perhaps he believed the Enterprise to be doomed from the start, and to avoid losing men in a hopeless project, had made haste with extreme slowness. Historians can only guess at why Philip, in bombarding Medina Sidonia with instructions, had never passed on any of this information.

Appalled by the news that Parma was not ready, and could not even give him the supplies he so badly needed,

The playing card above is true in spirit if not in fact: when Parma finally reached Dunkirk with his men, the Armada was already fighting—and losing—its last battle.

This contemporary painting shows the climactic moment at midnight on August 7, 1588, when eight fireships broke from the center of the English fleet (right) and bore down upon the Armada, massed under bare poles at left. In the foreground, the artist

has added a huge Spanish galleon fighting off an English ship (far left) and a galleass moving to attack one of Hawkins' new warships (right). In fact, the exploding fireships scattered the Armada in total confusion without a shot being fired.

121

Medina Sidonia sought help from the governor of Calais. He got a cold warning that his anchorage was a dangerous one—and a small basket of fruit as a sweetener.

Night closed down over the two fleets, with a fresh southwest wind that kept the ships rocking at their moorings. Then just after midnight, eight twinkling lights appeared from the midst of the English. They grew larger, flaring orange and crimson in the darkness, sending up showers of sparks. Borne by the wind and the inflowing tide, they came down headlong upon the Armada.

All the foreboding the Spaniards had felt seemed to come to a head. Spouting flames, and with their cannons crashing and bursting, the fireships drew near, "a horror to see in the night," as one Spanish officer wrote. These were the devil ships come again—terrible devices to blow them all to bits. The duke had posted pinnaces to fend them off, but the fireships got past this screen and came on. Medina Sidonia's orders were that if this happened

Although demoralized, the Armada escaped the fireships unharmed except for one galleass driven on shore under the walls of Calais. In this engraving by John Pine, Howard's squadron (at left) sends out its boats to board and loot the crippled vessel while the rest of the English fleet pursues the Armada, fleeing in the background.

his ships should slip their anchor cables and stand out to sea to let the fireships drift by. But in the panic most of the Spaniards cut their anchor cables clean through and fled. It was every ship for itself. At last, the splendid discipline of the Armada, which had held it in formation all through the days of fighting, went to pieces as ships bumped into one another in their frantic haste to escape. Not one was harmed by the fireships. But the English had "dislodged us with eight vessels," said a Spanish captain later, "something which they could not do with a hundred and thirty."

The first light of day on Monday, August 8, showed the Armada scattered away to the northeast before a steady wind. Following their battle plan, arranged the day before, the English moved into action. Lord Howard was to attack first, then Drake, then Hawkins, and lastly Frobisher, with Seymour's squadron supporting him. But this tactic was to be changed almost at once.

The leader of the galleasses, Hugo de Moncada's fine *San Lorenzo*, had collided with another ship during the wild alarm of the night. With her rudder smashed and her mainmast cracked, she had drifted to shore and lay stranded. This tempting prize was too much for Howard, and he turned aside with his squadron to capture her. The water was too shallow for the galleons, so the English put over their small boats, filled with sailors. There was a fierce fight in which Hugo de Moncada was killed by a musket ball through the head. Then Howard's men began looting the galleass until the governor of Calais, eager for a part in the plunder, turned the castle guns on them and sent them scurrying back to their ships.

While the Lord Admiral was busy with this distraction, Drake had followed his orders and gone on to chase the Spaniards. The *San Martin*, which had followed Medina Sidonia's instructions to slip cable and still had both anchors, had been lying hove to, to the northeast. With her were the few ships that had not panicked and still had their anchors left: five galleons in all. The duke fired a signal gun to summon the rest of his scattered flock. Then he and his little group prepared to engage the English,

OVERLEAF: *In this detail from the Vroom painting on pages 106–7 the English and the Spaniards jam their galleons' decks to fire muskets and shriek insults at one another. Although the slaughter on the Spanish ships was fearful, they bravely refused to surrender to "cowardly Lutheran hens."*
MRS. CATHERINE PALMER

With more enthusiasm than truth, these playing cards claim "More than halfe" the Armada sunk and gloat over the captured weapons "provided to destroy ye English."

falling back as they did so to give the rest of the Armada time to skirt the perilous sandbanks off Dunkirk and rally around their flagship.

The *San Martin* lay ready with her broadside guns loaded and run out as the *Revenge* drew nearer. Both ships waited, drifting closer and closer, for now roundshot was so scarce neither side could afford to waste it. At perhaps one hundred yards, Drake's guns went off, and a moment later the *San Martin* replied. The smoke rose high, stinging the eyes of the sailors. Shot crashed through the sides of both ships, wounding men with huge splinters as deadly as swords. Aboard the *Revenge* a wounded officer was afterwards said to have had his bed shot out from under him. "Sir Francis' ship," wrote a more straightforward chronicler, "was riddled with every kind of shot and was letting fly from both her broadsides so that she seemed to repeat her fire as rapidly as any soldier with a musket." Then the *Revenge* went past, and after her came the rest of Drake's squadron in line ahead, each ship loosing off her broadsides and bearing the *San Martin*'s return fire. Drake set a course for the northeast and sped away with his squadron following.

By this time Frobisher and his men had arrived to take their place. The *Triumph* engaged the *San Martin*, their guns keeping up a slow, heavy thunder. More of the Spanish warships sailed to help their admiral—de Leyva's big carrack, Bertendona's ship and Oquendo's, Recalde's scarred *San Juan*, some of the Portuguese and Castilian galleons. With the *San Martin* at the center, the crescent formed for the last time—only a thin line of perhaps twenty-five ships but containing most of Spain's fighting strength. For the first time they could engage the English unencumbered by storeships and slower craft. But so short of ammunition were they that, now the battle was finally at close quarters, they could not take full advantage of their heavy guns.

Hawkins appeared with his squadron and sailed in to join the battle. With him was Lord Henry Seymour and the Channel patrol, joyous at the chance of doing some fighting. And at last Lord Howard and his squadron arrived. Off to leeward, in the northeast, the bulk of the Armada had been trying to come downwind to rejoin Medina Sidonia, but Drake's squadron was driving a wedge between these ships and their commander, trying to run them aground on the shoals that lined the Dutch coast.

All day long the battle went on. And one by one the Spanish guns fell silent. Their ammunition had run out.

*The series of charts made by Robert Adams and Augustus Ryther to honor
Lord Howard ends with the English attack on the Armada off Calais.*

The August 8 battle was a scene of wild confusion as the English fought at close quarters for the first time, trying to drive the Armada onto the sandbanks off Flanders.

Many could only answer with musket fire. The English came in close, so that their lighter guns were really effective for the first time in the nine days of off-and-on battle. They still could not smash the heavy Spanish hulls, but they killed men, broke the lighter bulwarks and railings to bits, and brought masts and spars crashing down in a tangle of rigging. And in some cases they did pierce the thick oak planks, making holes large enough for the sea to rush in. In this way a greatship of Recalde's squadron was sunk, going down suddenly with 275 men aboard.

Again and again, Spanish ships tried to grapple their enemy, but the English sheered off and kept hammering at them, far more slowly now as they too ran out of powder and shot. A carrack—it may have been Bertendona's—was seen to swing around into the line of action with all her guns silenced, no shots coming from her save those of the musketeers, and as she heeled over before the wind, blood came pouring from her scuppers. A Portuguese galleon that had been in the thick of the fight began to settle lower in the water. Her captain managed to get her to shore, but there she was captured by Justin of Nassau and his men, who butchered her crew without mercy. Another galleon, the *San Felipe*, began to sink. One of the storeships offered to take off her captain, Don Francisco de Toledo, but he replied calmly that it looked better to go down in a galleon than a storeship, and he stayed with his ship. He too got his vessel to shore, only to lose her to the Sea Beggars.

Now Medina Sidonia could count at least four more fighting ships lost and many of the others dismasted or badly holed by the hammering they had so bravely taken. Over 600 men had been killed and 800 wounded—and many more were not included in the official count. In over a week of fighting, the Spaniards had fired 123,790 rounds of shot without putting one English ship out of action and killing, at the most, under 100 men.

The seas had been growing rougher and rougher, and about four o'clock a sudden squall blew up. The rain poured down violently, and the English hove to and shortened sail to keep from colliding with one another. When the rain had passed, they saw the Spaniards, with stubborn pride, once again formed up in battle order. But there was no more battle. Neither side had any ammunition left for a fight.

Elizabeth's victory medal bears, in Latin, the famous motto "God breathed and they were scattered."
THE MANSELL COLLECTION

Night closed in with high seas and a westerly gale that drove the battered Armada steadily toward the treacherous Zeeland banks. It seemed they must be doomed to run aground and the men perish either by drowning or at the hands of Justin of Nassau's Sea Beggars. With the first light of morning, Medina Sidonia's officers begged him to save himself and the holy standard by fleeing in a pinnace to a Spanish-held port on the mainland—Nieuport or Ostend. The duke, who had so far proved a much better commander than anyone had ever suspected, gallantly refused. All through the Spanish fleet men confessed and were shriven; only God could help them now.

And then, as it had so often before in the course of the battle, the wind changed. Blowing from the southwest, it bore the Spaniards safely away from the shoals and right out into the North Sea. The English followed, helpless to do anything but watch, yet ready for close combat if the Spaniards should turn and try to land in England. But the Spaniards did not turn.

God, in His mercy, had breathed, they claimed, in order to save them. But they little knew what lay in store. It was the English who were to pick up the phrase for a victory medal: "God breathed and they were scattered."

This painting of Elizabeth's procession to Tilbury also shows her giving thanks to God for defeating the Armada.

VII

THE LAST SHOTS FIRED

At a council held on board the battered *San Martin* that
Tuesday evening, August 9, Medina Sidonia and his captains voted, for the record, that they would turn back as
soon as the wind changed and try to fight their return passage through the Channel. But if it did not change within
four days, they would be forced to make their way home by
skirting around the north of Scotland and the Irish coastline far to the west. They had almost no ammunition left,
their casualties were heavy, and they were already running short of food and water.

The English fleet pursued them north under a following
wind until they reached the latitude of the Firth of Forth;
then, seeing that the Spaniards still held on their course
and did not turn aside to seek refuge with the Scots, Howard and his men turned about. They had to. On their ships
too, food and water were running so low that they were on
near-starvation rations. Two small swift ships followed the
Armada into the northern mists to keep watch until they
were sure the Spaniards could no longer attempt a landing.

Meanwhile, in England, hectic preparations were still
going on to meet the expected invasion. Since the beacons
first lit up the night sky on July 30, orders had gone out to
marshal the "trained bands" that were equivalent to a
militia and were Elizabeth's only defense against Parma's
seasoned troops. Although all the seacoast towns right up
to the Scottish border were on the alert, the main preparations were in the south of England, which was the most
likely spot for a landing. The Earl of Leicester, despite his
lack of success in the Netherlands, had been Elizabeth's
instant choice as captain general of her forces, and every
day fresh companies of volunteers were arriving at his headquarters at Tilbury in Kent, a few miles downriver from
London.

On Thursday, August 18, Elizabeth herself visited Tilbury to review her troops, who were paraded by regiments

An unknown Elizabethan artist dramatically combined the queen and her legions in a craggy, castle-dotted landscape (at left) with a tumultuous engagement on the seas.

to receive her. Careless of the risk she took in exposing herself so openly to any would-be assassin, she insisted on getting down from her horse and walking slowly through every quarter of the camp so that she could see her people and be seen by them. Of Elizabeth's many progresses through the land she loved so well, this was perhaps the most moving, and it inspired her to make a memorable speech:

I know I have the body of a weak and feeble woman, but I have the heart and stomach of a king, and of a king of England too, and think foul scorn that Parma or Spain, or any prince of Eu-

rope, should dare invade the borders of my realm; to which, rather than any dishonor shall grow by me, I myself will take up arms, I myself will be your general, judge, and rewarder of every one of your virtues in the field. I know already for your forwardness you deserve rewards and crowns, and we do assure you, in the word of a prince, they shall be duly paid you.

Brave words, but words are cheaper than coin. Although at the height of danger Elizabeth truly meant them, through the long weeks that followed she was far from being a rewarder. Howard and his captains brought back news of the Spaniards' flight, but the English, quite unaware how thoroughly demoralized and depleted the Armada was, were still not sure they had won a victory. They continued to be on the alert for the Armada to return and for Parma's men to arrive in their barges. Elizabeth and Burghley reluctantly had to keep both the trained-band army and the navy fully mobilized until September, when the danger at last seemed over.

But the English sailors could not be discharged until they were paid off, and, as usual, money was scarce. As a result, men stayed in their ships, where a raging epidemic was now taking a far more dreadful toll than any Spanish cannon balls. The Lord Admiral, desperate to help his men, pawned his personal valuables to pay as many as he

In this urgent letter, the English captains plan to "folowe . . . the Spanishe Fleete" until they clear the Firth of Forth, and the captains remind the queen that only want of supplies prevents the pursuit continuing "to the furthest that they durste have gone." Lord Howard's signature is first; "Fra: Drake" and "John Hawkyns" follow.

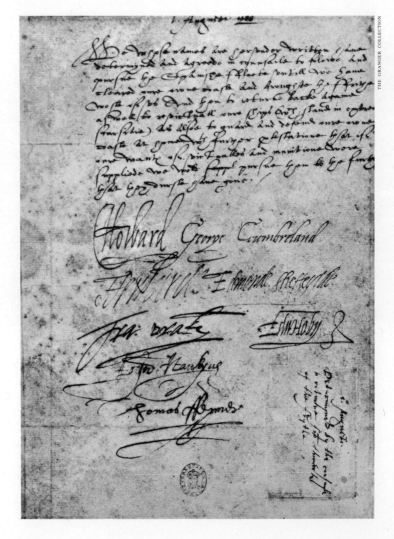

could and appropriated the money Drake had taken from the *Rosario* for extra funds. "I did take . . . 3,000 pistolets," he wrote to Walsingham, "for, by Jesus, I had not £3 besides in the world, and had not anything [that] could get money in London; and I do assure you my plate was gone before. . . . But if I had not some to have bestowed upon some poor and miserable men, I should have wished myself out of this world." Hawkins, endlessly preparing lists of expenditures for the queen and Walsingham, wrote despairingly: "My pain and misery in this service is infinite . . . God, I trust, will deliver me of it ere long, for there is no other hell."

But there was another hell, and the Spaniards were enduring it.

They had taken the long, cold road home. Every man in the fleet was on a daily ration of half a pound of bread, one pint of water, and half a pint of wine, all that was fit to use of the stores they had carried so far. In order to conserve water, they had thrown their horses and mules overboard, never thinking that they could have been slaughtered for fresh meat. Their holds were full of wounded and fever-ridden men, and every day saw more burials at sea.

For safety they swung in a wide arc between the Orkney and Shetland islands, keeping well out to sea beyond the Hebrides, off the west coast of Scotland, and down toward Ireland. Wild storms battered them, dispersing the fleet little by little. Seventeen ships at least were wrecked on the Irish coast, where half-savage peasants and fishermen robbed the living and the dead alike of everything they had. On one beach alone more than a thousand bodies were washed up, and the wreckage of ships' timbers was strewn for five miles. By order of the English Lord Deputy of Ireland, nearly all the unfortunate Spaniards who were captured alive were massacred to prevent any chance of their raising the Catholic Irish in rebellion. A few hundred eventually made their way home after terrible privations.

Of all those haughty ships that had sailed so confidently out of Lisbon, only half got home again. And of the great captains of Spain who had led the Armada, only a handful survived the year.

Recalde put into the Irish coast for water and managed to escape again. In October he reached Corunna, getting out of his sickbed to direct the helmsman into port. But he was mortally ill, and before the end of the month he was dead. Bold young Alonso de Leyva was drowned with 1,300 men near the Giant's Causeway in a last desperate attempt

Spanish ships cast away on the Irish Shoare with Marriners and Seamen

The west coast of Ireland was the Armada's graveyard. Seventeen ships sank along its rocky shore.

OVERLEAF: *Exquisitely detailed sea monsters rise out of the spray in Cornelisz Vroom's painting of the Armada's terrible voyage through the northern waters. Vroom, the first great marine artist, probably painted this picture around 1600.*

Queene Eliz: Riding in Triumph through London in a Chariot drawn by two Horses and all ye Companies attending her with their Baners

Queene Eliz: wth Nobles and Gentry and a great number of people giving God humble thanks in St Pauls Church. and having set upp the Ensignes taken from the Spaniards.

On December 4, 1588, Elizabeth went in solemn procession through the London streets to St. Paul's Cathedral to kneel and thank God for the Spaniards' defeat. Both events are shown on Armada cards.

to reach the Scottish coast. Oquendo, the Glory of the Fleet, had left his squadron after the final battle north of Calais. It was said that Medina Sidonia called to him then, "What shall we do? We are lost!" and that he replied, "I am going to fight and die like a man," and ordered his ship away. He too came home in October and was dead, from heartbreak and sickness, by November. Pedro de Valdes, who had surrendered to Drake, spent four and a half years as a prisoner in England; fiery Hugo de Moncada had died in the defense of his galleass.

Of the chief officers, only Bertendona, Diego Flores de Valdes, and Medina Sidonia himself saw the next year in Spain. Bertendona was to face an English raid the following year and burn his ship in harbor rather than surrender her. Diego Flores, everybody's scapegoat for the Armada's failure, spent some time in prison.

As for Medina Sidonia, he brought home the *San Martin*, and forty-four more ships with her, early in September, and other survivors straggled in as fall drew into winter. But many of the vessels were too battered and bruised ever to fight again, and for weeks the pitiful remnant of their crews went on dying from sickness and starvation.

Broken in health and worn out from the terrible journey and the weight of his responsibilities, Medina Sidonia wrote to the king blaming himself for the failure of the Enterprise. Others condemned him too, although he had done better than many a more experienced commander might have in his place. The king, at least, did not reproach him but permitted him to retire to his estates to rest and recuperate. He lived on to serve Philip and his son, Philip III, for another twenty years, but the ghosts of the Armada must have haunted him to the end of his days.

England celebrated what had finally turned out to be a victory with ringing church bells and special holidays. The queen attended a service of thanksgiving at St. Paul's in London, at which the captured Spanish banners were displayed. In giving thanks to God for their deliverance, the English should have thanked their sailors too, for the victory had been chiefly due to the superiority of their new design of ships and guns.

Almost at once, however, squabbles broke out among the captains. Frobisher accused Drake of cowardice and self-seeking. Seymour complained that he had been kept too long in the Channel. John Hawkins worried about his beloved ships, which needed repairs. Lord Howard worried about their crews. Only Drake kept his spirits high; he

*In this water color of the "Wilde Irische,"
a sixteenth-century Dutch artist portrays
a typical pair of inhabitants of the bleak,
inhospitable country where many Armada
vessels and their crews ended the campaign.*

was already busy planning another move against Spain.

Drake's scheme has been called the English Armada, although it was in fact another private venture, and only a few ships belonged to the queen. There were sixty Dutch vessels, sixty armed English merchantmen, and six fine greatships of the royal navy. All were under Drake's command. With him was Sir John Norris, a famous soldier, at the head of an army of nearly 15,000 men. In Drake's charge once again was Don Antonio de Crato, the would-be king of Portugal, making one more bid to wrest the crown from King Philip.

The plan was that this huge fleet—fully as many sail as had been in the Enterprise against England—would first destroy in their harbors those ships that had survived the Armada, then land on the coast of Portugal, near Lisbon, and make an attempt to put Don Antonio on the throne. Don Antonio was positive that the Portuguese would rise in his support. But if they did not, Drake might then try to capture the Azores.

This fleet was almost as ill-fated as the Spanish Armada had been. The weather, on which all the luck of sailing ships depended, was against them. For eleven days the fleet stayed in harbor, consuming the provisions already stored on board. When at last they did sail, in June, 1589, they went, not to Santander, where forty Armada vessels lay, but to Corunna, where there was only one, Bertendona's *San Juan*, and he, swearing to be revenged, burned her himself. After a grim fight they took the town but got little profit from it. By the time they reached Lisbon, the Portuguese had closed their gates and refused to consider accepting Don Antonio as king. The fleet never did get to the Azores—terrible storms parted the ships from one another. Wounds and disease thinned their ranks so severely that some 8,000 men were lost. Drake returned to England to face the queen's anger. The expedition had been disorganized and poorly handled. Its mission had been to destroy the Spanish ships, and Drake had ignored this in order to seek plunder instead. He was disgraced, and it was six years before he again held a command.

The long war between England and Spain dragged on. It was not so much a war as a series of independent battles, as English privateers tried to capture Spanish treasure ships or the queen hurried to help the Dutch and French Protestants in opposing Philip on land.

In the summer of 1589 Henry III of France was murdered, and Henry of Navarre succeeded him as Henry IV. The Catholic Holy League, which had sworn it would never acknowledge a Protestant as king, called upon Philip of Spain to act as its protector. He agreed, bringing men from

As the Holy League, controlled by the Duke of Guise and financed by Philip, increased its power, terrifying processions be-

140

the Netherlands to strengthen the French league's armies. For another five years civil war continued in France, until in 1593 all the moderate parties united in begging Henry to change his religion and unify their divided country once more. Remarking dryly that "Paris was well worth a mass," he did so, and ended forever Philip's hopes of taking over France. By withdrawing Parma's troops to support the Holy League, the king had fatally weakened Parma at a time when he might at last have been successful in overcoming Dutch resistance. The Spanish hold on the Netherlands too would soon be gone.

However, Philip had indeed taken a lesson from the defeat of the Armada. He began to build up a Spanish navy that would be a disciplined, potent force instead of a motley collection of ships from different countries. Since his ability to do this depended on revenue from the New World, he increased the efforts of his treasure fleets. Consequently, England tried one plan after another to intercept the flow of wealth between the West Indies and Spain. Hawkins suggested a blockade, which failed to work chiefly because the queen would not support it for a long enough period. Keeping relays of ships at sea was too expensive for her limited resources.

In 1595 Drake made one more of his audacious proposals. This was to try another stroke at the very heart of Spain's riches—to land an army at Nombre de Dios, capture Panama, and hold the isthmus for the queen.

If the venture had succeeded, it might have had a greater effect on the course of history than the defeat of the Armada. But it had been twenty years since Drake led his lively band of young men in search of Spanish gold. Spain now had a large army in that region, and Philip's

gan parading through the streets of French cities seeking out Huguenots to kill in order to bolster the Catholics' strength.

newly built, well-armed ships constantly patrolled the Caribbean. And the queen fatally weakened the expedition by making sure that her instructions would be heeded this time: Drake was to share his command equally with John Hawkins.

In September, 1595, the old shipmates sailed once more for the Spanish Main. Hawkins was old, tired, and touchy. Drake, with the years, had become even more arrogant and difficult to deal with. The two quarreled from the start. Drake had overcrowded his flagship with men, and he asked Hawkins to take some. Hawkins, who as usual had carefully regulated both men and provisions on board his ship, angrily refused. "The fire which lay hid in their stomachs," said one of their captains, Thomas Maynarde, "began to break forth, and had not the colonel pacified them, it would have grown further." The colonel was

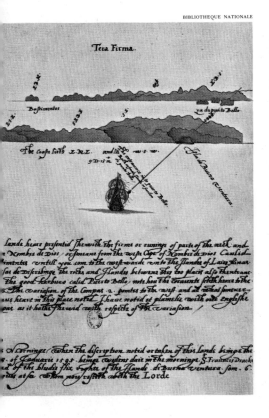

These 1591 portraits of Drake (left) and Hawkins (right) honor their contribution to the defeat of the Armada. Above, the log of their voyage together four years later, on which Hawkins died, sadly notes Drake's death too.

Thomas Baskerville, a veteran commander, who was in charge of the troops in the fleet.

The expedition's first objective was to capture the flagship of the treasure fleet, which, they knew, had been dismasted in a storm and was lying in the harbor of San Juan, Puerto Rico, waiting for a Spanish convoy to escort her to Seville. She had two million ducats aboard, which could be theirs if they got there before her escort.

But Drake, eager for extra profit and anxious to find provisions for his hungry crew, insisted that they visit the Canary Islands on the way. Unwillingly, because of the inevitable delay, Hawkins agreed. But the local Spanish soldiery captured the English landing parties, Drake had to head for the West Indies with no extra supplies, and Hawkins was forced to share his provisions after all. Worse still, the English prisoners let slip the expedition's destination, and the Spaniards were able to prepare a welcome.

The English appeared off San Juan on November 22, 1595, and the fortress guns at once roared out. One shot broke the mizzenmast of Drake's ship, the *Defiance*; a second smashed through the wall of his cabin and killed two officers. The English had to move out of range, with several dead and wounded.

But they had suffered an even worse loss. John Hawkins had not been well when he left England; by the morning of their arrival at Puerto Rico he was dying. At San Juan de Ulua, in Mexico, he had seen the first sharp crisis of the war. Now, at another San Juan, he looked from his cabin window upon one of its last moments. He dictated a codicil to his will, leaving his queen two thousand pounds "to make the best amends," as he said, for the fact that he had persuaded her to venture her ships in such a calamity. Before the Spanish guns opened up, Hawkins was dead.

Philip II, whose splendid tomb in the Escorial is seen below, found death a merciful release from gout, which tormented him even when he sat in the special chair above.

For the next two days, Drake tried to win San Juan, but it was too strong for him. "I will bring thee to twenty places far more wealthy and easier to be gotten," he insisted, and ordered his fleet to sail for Panama.

At Nombre de Dios, on the eastern side of the Isthmus, he landed Colonel Baskerville and his troops. But the Spaniards had built a stockade across the road to Panama, and they defended it vigorously. Baskerville had to retreat to the ships, leaving Nombre de Dios in flames behind him.

The fleet now sailed northward, but the wind was contrary, and the ships had to anchor and wait for it to change. Men began to sicken and die of dysentery, and Drake himself caught the disease. He took to his cabin, growing weaker daily. The Indies had changed from "a delicious and pleasant arbor" to "a vast and desert wilderness," he groaned to Maynarde. His mind wandered, and gold filled his thoughts. "I know many means to do Her Majesty good service and to make us rich!" he raved.

Giving up hope of a southerly wind, the fleet sailed back to Panama. On the evening of February 5, 1596, Drake crawled out of bed and dressed himself. He was delirious, and no one could understand what he said. With difficulty they got him back to bed. The *Defiance* dropped anchor in Portobelo Bay, and the next morning, "quietly in his cabin," at the age of about fifty-four, he died. He was buried at sea in a leaden coffin, and Colonel Baskerville took charge of the "sorrowful voyage" that had been the final one for two great sailors.

That spring, as Baskerville was arriving in England, Lord Howard set forth with a huge English fleet for Cadiz. He sailed into Cadiz Bay, answering the batteries with defiant trumpet blasts; then his soldiers stormed the town and took it. It was a victory, but a hollow one, for the Spanish commander—ironically enough, it was the Duke of Medina Sidonia—burned more than fifty merchant ships with their valuable cargoes rather than see them fall into English hands.

Later that year, King Philip tried to retaliate by sending another Armada against England, but storms drove it out of the Channel. Yet again, in 1597, he sent out a fleet, but it too was scattered by gales. The following year, the worn-out king made all the arrangements for his own funeral, down to the ordering of the correct amount of black cloth in which to drape his chapel, and then, with every detail taken care of, he died.

When Queen Elizabeth followed him in 1603, she had

Forced to leave Panama, scene of Drake's early successes, with no treasure and with his great captain dying, Colonel Baskerville burned the city of Nombre de Dios (above).

named as her heir James VI of Scotland, the son of Mary Queen of Scots. As James I, he united the two kingdoms for the first time. The days of Spain's predominance were already over. The new king, Philip III, had inherited his father's problems: the crumbling of Spain's empire and an empty treasury. James of England was able to sign a treaty with Philip that officially ended their countries' long conflict and to make new alliances with the Netherlands and France that effectively prevented Spain from ever again becoming the chief power in Europe.

The defeat of the Armada had been the pivot on which the struggle between the Catholic and the Protestant nations turned. Already the German Protestant princes were challenging Catholic authority, and Europe stood on the threshold of another religious war that would last more than thirty years. As the week-long battle with the mighty fleet of Spain became matter for old men's reminiscences, Englishmen began to think of it as the crowning event in Elizabeth's long reign—a glorious victory worthy of a queen who had been called Gloriana. With it, the era of crusading had in fact gone by forever. A more cynical and more practical attitude to politics was to take over as the balance of world power shifted and Spain yielded pride of place to the growing empire of France.

The independence that the Dutch had won they kept, and the Netherlands formally became a separate nation in 1609. The Sea Beggars were the forerunners of a magnificent navy whose daring captains set up the flag of empire in the Pacific Ocean and helped plant Dutch colonies in the East Indies.

England had shown the world the strength of her ships and a new pattern of naval warfare. Inevitably, her future was now committed to the ocean. Although Drake and Hawkins and their comrades had been turned back from Spain's new world, Englishmen were to follow other leaders westward and to plant colonies at last in the new world of the North American continent. The restless, daring spirit that brought a flood of ships out of one small island to seek their future on the high seas was to find lodging in America, and in the end to change the face and nature of the world.

This Armada portrait of the queen called Gloriana depicts Elizabeth, in a gown encrusted with magnificent jewels, standing between two paintings: at left is the victorious English fleet; at right is the defeated Armada.

PERMISSION OF THE TRUSTEES OF THE BRITISH MUSEUM

This sixteenth-century engraving shows a seaman in the tall hat and baggy trousers that would become the first English naval uniform.

AMERICAN HERITAGE
PUBLISHING CO., INC.

James Parton, *President*
Richard M. Ketchum, *Editorial Director, Book Division*
Stephen W. Sears, *Editor, Education Department*
Irwin Glusker, *Art Director*

HORIZON CARAVEL BOOKS
JOSEPH L. GARDNER, *Managing Editor*
Janet Czarnetzki, *Art Director*
Jean Atcheson, *Associate Editor*
Elaine K. Andrews, *Copy Editor*
Laurie B. Platt, *Picture Researcher*
Gertrudis Feliu, *Chief, European Bureau*
Claire de Forbin, *European Bureau*

ACKNOWLEDGMENTS

The Editors are particularly grateful for the valuable assistance of Mrs. Mary Jenkins in London. In addition, they would like to thank the following individuals and organizations:

The Duke of Alba
Archivo MAS, Barcelona
Biblioteca Nacional, Madrid
British Museum—L. W. Coulson
British Travel Association—Marion Jennings
Mrs. Jane de Cabanyes, Madrid
City Museum and Art Gallery, Plymouth—A. A. Cumming
Ferdinand Museum, Innsbruck
Folger Shakespeare Library, Washington, D.C.—Mrs. Elaine W. Fowler
Hispanic Society of America, New York—Mrs. Eleanor S. Font
Magdalene College, Cambridge—G. D. Pepys Whiteley
Musées Royaux des Beaux-Arts, Brussels
Museo Naval, Madrid
National Maritime Museum, Greenwich—Edward H. H. Archibald, Mrs. E. Tucker
New York Public Library, Rare Book Division—Mrs. Maud Cole
Rijksmuseum, Amsterdam
Stichting Johan Maurits van Nassau, The Hague—A. V. D. Vaart

FURTHER REFERENCE

For those who would like to know more about the Armada and the lives of the people concerned with it, the following books are suggested:

Corbett, Julian S., *Drake and the Tudor Navy*, 2 vols. Longmans, Green, 1898.

Davies, R. Trevor, *The Golden Century of Spain, 1501–1621*. St. Martin's, 1954.

Elliott, J. H., *Imperial Spain, 1469–1716*. St. Martin's, 1964.

Froude, J. A., *The Spanish Story of the Armada*. Scribner's, 1892.

Lewis, Michael, *The Spanish Armada*. Macmillan, 1960.

Mason, A. E. W., *Sir Francis Drake*. Doubleday, 1941.

Mattingly, Garrett, *The Armada*. Houghton Mifflin, 1959.

————*The "Invincible" Armada and Elizabethan England*. Cornell University Press, 1963.

McKee, Alexander, *From Merciless Invaders*. Norton, 1964.

Neale, J. E., *Queen Elizabeth I*. Doubleday, 1957.

Nicoll, Allardyce, *The Elizabethans*. Cambridge University Press, 1957.

Petrie, Charles A., *Philip II of Spain*. Norton, 1963.

Rowse, A. L., *The England of Elizabeth*. Macmillan, 1951.

Unwin, Rayner, *The Defeat of John Hawkins*. Macmillan, 1960.

Williamson, James A., *The Age of Drake*. Barnes & Noble, 1960.

————*The Tudor Age*. McKay, 1958.

Woodroffe, Thomas, *Vantage at Sea*. St. Martin's, 1958.

INDEX

Bold face indicates pages on which maps or illustrations appear

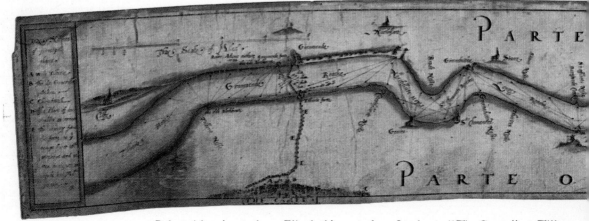

Robert Adams' map shows Elizabeth's route from London to "The Campe" at Tilbury

(left) down a Thames bristling with gun positions and booms to block a Spanish attack.